NORTHUS SHETLAND CLASSICS

‡

Northus Shetland Classics is a series of reprints of some of the keystones of Shetland's literature. The series has been established under the guiding eye of noted poet and novelist Robert Alan Jamieson, and operates with the assistance of an advisory group of local academics and writers. Each volume has an introduction by an expert. Works in Shetlandic and English, and those which combine the two, will be included. The series is divided into four streams:

Poyims / Poetry

Alting / Non-Fiction

Myndins / Memoir

Yarns / Fiction

This volume is dedicated to the memory of Alex Cluness, poet and activist for Shetland literature who dreamt of just such a series of reprints, and whose own family had its origins in the beautiful isle of Unst.

BROKEN LIGHTS

Poems and Reminiscences of the Late Basil Ramsay Anderson

‡

Northus Shetland Classics

Poyims

TITLES IN THIS SERIES

already published

Tang J. J. Haldane Burgess

Broken Lights Basil Ramsay Anderson

forthcoming

Foula: Island West of the Sun Sheila Gear

Letters on Shetland Peter Jamieson

Rock-Bound Jessie Saxby

BROKEN LIGHTS

Poems and Reminiscences of the Late Basil Ramsay Anderson

edited by

JESSIE M. E. SAXBY

‡

introduced by

Robert Alan Jamieson

NORTHUS
SHETLAND
CLASSICS

Broken Lights first published 1888 by R & R Clark, Edinburgh
and C & A Sandison, Lerwick

Introduction first published in this edition
Introduction © Robert Alan Jamieson 2021

This edition published 2021 by

Michael Walmer

North House

Melby

Sandness

Shetland, ZE2 9PL

ISBN 978-0-6489204-7-2 paperback

CONTENTS

INTRODUCTION *Robert Alan Jamieson*..............................i

IN MEMORIAM

BASIL RAMSAY ANDERSON *Jessie M. E. Saxby et al*...........xxi

BROKEN LIGHTS *Jessie M. E. Saxby*..............................lv

POEMS IN ENGLISH AND SCOTS

NICHT-FA'..3

A VIGIL...5

WORK AND SONG..6

THE OLD ROCK...8

HONEST OLÉ..11

COME, GATHER THE WEALTH OF THE WAVE...........15

"DEATH TO THE HEAD THAT WEARS NO HAIR".........18

TWILIGHT...20

THE HERRING KING...24

THE FURTHER HAAF...27

THE MARINER'S DEATH……………………………………29

I SIGH FOR THE ISLES……………………………………30

MAGNIE'S AWA'……………………………………………32

A FOUR-YEAR-OLD…………………..……………………34

THE OLD MAN…………………………………………......40

THE ISLES OF THE NORD………………………………....45

UPWARD………………………………………………….48

SHETLAND HOSPITALITY………………………………..50

TO A LERWICK LASS……………………………………52

THE DARKENED LAMP………………………………….....56

A CRY FROM THE POOR……………………………..…….60

NIGHT……………………………………………..…………63

CLOUD AND STAR……………………………….………66

NIGHT THOUGHTS………………………………...……..68

THE BUSY STREET………………………………………69

LICHTSOME HEART………………………………...…….75

SUNSET………………………………………….……......77

NIGHT SHADES…………………………………..……….80

ALONE………………………………………..…………..82

"GOD IS OUR DEFENCE"…………………………..………84

THE BOOK……………………………………...………….87

THE NORTH WIND...88

TRUTH...90

THE MERMAID'S SONG.............................92

AN ANGEL OF THE NETHER BLUE................97

AN OLD SONG...101

OLD AND NEW...104

TWO BUDS...106

A LOVER'S DREAM...107

A TRUE MAN...108

RECOGNITION...110

A FAREWELL...113

A HIDDEN GEM...114

A BONNIE FACE...116

THE SPELL OF THE SEA.................................118

PRESENT YET PAST...120

POEMS IN THE SHETLAND DIALECT

FRAGMENT ADDRESSED TO HIS MOTHER.............125

AULD MAUNSIE'S CRÜ.................................126

IRONBONNS, DA MAN O' MICHT.....................137

STROOPIE I 'DA ASE...142

COMIN' FAE DA HILL..145

FRAM...147

HEIM-FOLK..149

DA RESTIN' O' DA FIRE..151

THE LADDIE HE WAS BLATE................................153

THE SNELL WINDS ARE BLAWIN'.........................157

LIVIN' COLLS AN' CAULD CLODS.........................160

DA TWININ' O'T..161

EXTRACTS FROM LETTERS

TO HIS BROTHER PETER......................................167

TO HIS FRIEND CHARLES NICOL.........................181

GLOSSARY OF SHETLAND TERMS

Gilbert Goudie

NOTE..185

GLOSSARY..188

NOTES TO THE SECOND EDITION *R.A. Jamieson*..........213

INTRODUCTION

The text of the book that follows first appeared in Edinburgh in 1888 – the year of a crofters' riot in Lewis, of the first Old Firm game, the International Exhibition of Science, Art and Industry at Kelvingrove Park in Glasgow, and the founding of the Scottish Labour Party. Of Jack the Ripper, and the race to the north between competing railways on the London-Edinburgh line. In Scottish literature, it was the era of Robert Louis Stevenson, indeed, of William McGonagall, and the emergence of J. M. Barrie and the 'Kailyard School' that would dominate the scene for a generation. Shetland was then in its 'herring boom', and the British Empire was in its pomp.

Broken Lights is a commemorative volume, gathering the work of a young poet who had died in January that year, of 'consumption' at the age of 26 — one of a Shetland family, exiled in Leith, which had already seen tragedy. The book's editor was a fellow Shetlander, an older woman, the first truly professional writer from the isles. She was one of the outstanding Edmondston family from Unst — Jessie — who had married a doctor, Henry Saxby, and left Shetland. Following her husband's early death, she supported her family through a vast range of prolific writings, and in Edinburgh was central to the 'ex-pat' Shetland community there, as president of the Edinburgh Orkney & Shetland Association, before returning to Unst to enjoy a long and active old age. But more of Jessie Saxby in subsequent volumes of the series, where she will appear as author herself.

Leith, being a port, and where the first regular ferry service to the isles ran from in the early nineteenth century, was where the majority of Shetlanders in the Edinburgh area had congregated — around the time of the book's publication, half a century on, Prince Regent Street was known as 'Shetlanders'

Avenue', as a resident once told me. But beyond that maritime locus by the port, the Shetland community was spread across Edinburgh, and included some eminent figures in the city's life, such as Gilbert Goudie, the antiquarian, who provides a glossary of Shetland words here. A number of them, including Goudie, contribute remembrances of the recently deceased young poet they had come to know — Basil Ramsay Anderson — and we are certainly indebted to "Mrs. Saxby" even now for having assembled this book to preserve not only Anderson's poetry, but also the memory of who he was to those who knew him.

Yet the book *Broken Lights*, as a whole, does even more valuable archival work — it preserves something of that Shetland community as it existed in Leith and Edinburgh in 1888, in the reminiscences and Basil's own letters. A community still closely connected to the isles, and to their fellow exiles, meeting for worship and for social events, keeping the old traditions alive — and, for the poets among them, of which there were a few, an audience for poems and songs about their homeland, often, though not exclusively by any means, in the native dialect they all shared.

This was the world that Anderson knew from the age of 14, the one in which the poet developed and matured. Prior to that, when he first penned verse in school exercise books, the family lived on the isle of Unst, as Saxby explains. I need not pre-empt her excellent account of the tragedy that befell the family, but it is clear from Anderson's poetry, with its recurrent imagery of loss at sea, that he was deeply affected by it. Nor need I give the poet a character here, for that is also excellently done by those whose tributes follow.

I can, though, offer a little more information on the poet's family, in terms of its origins, thanks to the internet age, in particular to the excellent Bayanne family history site. While Basil Anderson was born on the 6th of August 1861 at Wasterhouse in Caldback, Unst, his mother's island home, his father hailed from Uralie in the island of Yell. Tracing their families, we find that Elizabeth Ramsay's line — Basil's mother to whom he was so attached — goes back to a marriage between a Ramsay man and an Unst woman, Ursula Isbister, sometime in the early eighteenth century. On his father's side, the Andersons, we can trace his lineage back further, through various patronymic changes, to a John Manson from Fetlar who established himself at Basta in Yell in the 1600s, where the family subsequently lived for generations.

Peter Anderson and Elizabeth Ramsay married on the 20th of December 1855, and by the 7th of August 1866, the day of his untimely death, they already had five children – a daughter would follow. Besides Basil, the third, of particular note are his two younger brothers, Peter to whom he addresses some of his letters, and Andrew who had died from consumption just a few months before Basil, as Saxby recounts; and his younger sister Mary Ann, who adds her voice to the commemorative tributes here, and would herself die young in 1891. These four of the family all succumbed to TB.

We can chart, via the 1881 census, Elizabeth's removal with her children to Edinburgh, where they appear as living at 11 Market Place, St Cuthberts, and she is listed as a 'Knitter of Shetland Hosiery'. Basil, when well enough, was employed as a lawyer's clerk. From there they would move to 12 Albert Street in Leith, where Basil died on the 7th of January, 1888.

I can also add a note of 'future' genealogy, something Saxby could not have known, which is that the daughter of Basil's younger brother Peter — who went to live with his family in Montrose, and took their mother there to live with them — grew up to be an important figure in 20th century Scottish literature. Willa Anderson, one of the first women graduates of St Andrews University, married the Orcadian writer Edwin Muir, and went on to produce a substantial body of work, including two fine novels, as Willa Muir. It's tempting to surmise that the sense of importance attached to education which drove the young Unst widow, Elizabeth Anderson, to send her fatherless children to school, no matter what, inspiring Basil to become a 'pupil teacher' there, might also have inspired the young Willa to further her studies — as the sage wisdom of a live-in grandmother, rather than a devoted mother. Regardless, there can be little doubt that Willa would have been well-acquainted with the first edition of *Broken Lights* in her Montrose home.

Besides this historical contextualising, what I might usefully do here is consider the poetry itself, as this was perhaps a lesser concern for those in 1888 who had recently lost a friend, and wanted to record his presence for posterity. By all accounts, he was a splendid fellow, good company, a Radical and a Christian, but he was also a prolific young writer, who took his craft seriously, as one friend notes.

It is suggested by Mrs. Saxby herself that her young protégé's writing in English was not of the standard of his work in the Shetland dialect. I feel that is more a reflection of the high quality of his dialect writing, rather than a condemnation of his work in English. In fact, his work in English and in Scots displays the same gift for rhythm, and an ease with rhyme, as his Shetland poetry. If the English diction is often formal, seemingly antiquated to our ears, it is of its period, and shows the markers of accepted poetic diction in the era of Tennyson, the Brownings (name-checked in 'Upward'), Longfellow and so forth — though it might be noted that for a Shetlander who knew the difference between familiar and formal forms of the second pronoun from the dialect, to use 'thy' and 'thou' and 'thine' is not unnaturally affected.

Anderson is, I feel, a better 'non-Shetland' poet than his peers, and later critics such as William J. Tait, seem to give him credit for, if we read the work in period and in context. A number of poems, such as 'A Cry from the Poor', fuse

Christian and Radical themes to powerful effect. Others such as 'Lichtsome Heart' display a Burnsian spirit – Burns, "The sweetest singer of the West— / The truest Bard, I trow—" ('Work and Song'). These Lowland Scots verses mark Anderson out as a writer in three tongues, not simply English and the Shetland, and are the product, no doubt, of his twelve years in exile, the voices he heard around him. He may, as some dialect poets do, have wondered if, by writing in something closer to Scots, or in English, he might reach a wider audience.

While some of the poems collected here are clearly more ephemeral, and may not have seen publication under other circumstances — being more juvenile exercises in verse as Tait suggests, prompted by some event or taking the form of intimate communication to another individual — even in these occasional pieces I still find an ear for the musicality of poetry that is fundamentally 'true'; and he is also capable of casting memorable images on the reader's mind, even when dealing with more trivial themes, such as in his paean to the isles in 'To a Shetland Lass': "…. Lerwick, like a fair maid, dips / Her bare feet in the sea". Note how cleverly he evokes 'da lodberries' here.

Juvenile some of these verses may be, but this is a gifted juvenile. If, as is claimed in what follows in the text of *Broken Lights*, he knew little of poetry beyond a few treasured books, his gift is possibly the poetic equivalent of 'perfect pitch'; a natural feeling for the medium, its cadences and rhythms, which education can't provide, nor entirely compensate for, if it is absent. Though this may be to underestimate the work the poet has done to achieve the effect, Anderson's poetry, however crafted and revised, has line by line a sense of rhythmic ease which seems natural.

All that said, some defence of the quality of the English writing having been duly made — and, it should again be noted, of the poems in Scots which lean towards Shetland speech but are not included in the final section of dialect poems — the Shetland part of the book is where I would suggest the reader begins; read the Scots and English poetry later, or even not at all. For it is these few wondrous Shetland 'poyims', only twelve in number, largely in 'da dialect' of his native Unst, that makes Basil Ramsay Anderson a name revered even now among Shetlanders — and prime among that twelve is 'Auld Maunsie's Crü'.

William Sandison, in *Shetland Verse: Remnants of the Norn* (1952), observed that:

> ... Anderson wrote most naturally, exactly the way he would have talked when among his own people ... His dialect is simple, with no pretence at any great knowledge of the Norn, what words he used falling unconsciously from his pen as they would, in speech, have fallen from his lips. He was a born poet with the instincts of a dramatist ... He died, perhaps, before he attained his full strength as a poet, but he left behind him "Auld Maunsie's Krö" (sic), which

is to Shetland crofter life what 'The Cottar's Saturday Night' is to Lowland Scottish …

And yes, if any single poem stands as Shetland's earliest dialect masterpiece, Anderson's opus has a strong claim. It is a powerful meditation on time's passage and humanity's labour, and marvellously suggestive, in its conclusion, of misinterpretation and myth, all executed in a perfectly cadenced Shetland dialect. It is notable also as a kind of myth-making itself, in the creation of an archetypal figure in the crofter/fisherman, Maunsie, attuned to nature, inheritor of the legacy of the independent settler, the *udaler* of old. As Laurence Graham writes in his essay 'Shetland Literature and the idea of community', in *Shetland's Northern Links: Language and History* (1996):

> … his masterpiece … is about an old Unst crofter and his crö, how he built it and how as well as providing food for him and his livestock, it became a noted landmark, a mied [navigation-point] at sea, even a time-piece for the folk round about and a shelter for sheep, cattle and ponies … the whole development of the poem is beautifully shaped. It unfolds in ever-widening

circles around the centre point of the crö, like ripples on a pond. It describes in turn the cycle of a typical crofting day from dawn to dusk, then the cycle of the seasons, next with Auld Maunsie's death — a human life come full circle. And finally the cycle not only of the years, but of the generations ...

Mark Ryan Smith, in his ground-breaking account *The Literature of Shetland* (2014), provides an excellent reading of the poem, its themes and structure, and ends by assessing it as:

> ... a kailyard poem which is anything but Kailyard in its execution. Negotiating skilfully between abstract images and ideas, and a very rooted, practical, down-to-earthness, Anderson's poem is one of the most complex and intelligently crafted Shetland poems. It is a significant reference point for what can be done in the local language and represents a coming of age and an evolutionary leap in Shetland's literature.

The achievement is self-evident — his 'masterpiece', as Smith rightly says, is itself a kind of 'mied' for later Shetland writers like myself – a work in which the kailyard is not a literary style, but a physical entity where kail can be grown, developed symbolically and even metaphysically in the poem.

All the same, personally, I like to read 'Auld Maunsie's Crü' as one of a suite of twelve, or rather a fragment plus eleven, as presented here by Mrs. Saxby. If this is the major poem among them, as it undoubtedly is, the more minor are no less tuneful and beautiful in their different keys; the complementary effect is fine, and I like many of the others very much, individually. But taken together, in their range and their reach, they are sublime — a *peerie* Shetland treasure in the grand story of world literature.

Thanks to Mrs. Saxby's work as editor, we are able to form a picture of the author, and so, to hear or read these Shetland poems as the inner voices of home calling to a young exile haunted by TB, missing his own familiar people while attempting to navigate the pavements of a strange urban world — an alienation that finds expression in the English poem, 'The Busy Street': "Where thousands meet and never greet, / How lone and cold is the busy street!" Interestingly, Basil Anderson's experience of exile prefigures in part that of the man his niece Willa would later marry, Edwin Muir, who was taken from his childhood island home of Wyre in Orkney at the same age, but to Glasgow, rather than Edinburgh. Willa herself is recorded as regarding her own Shetland family in Montrose as 'D.P.'s', war-time jargon for 'displaced persons', who spoke Shetland dialect, the cause of mockery among her friends as a small girl. Like her uncle, she knew three tongues: Shetland, Montrose Scots, and the English of school; and in her later life she attributed her gift with languages to this beginning.

We are indeed indebted to Mrs. Saxby. However, the credit given her notwithstanding, she was not without critics for her editorial work, and thanks to the archivist Brian Smith I am informed that Basil's brother Robert — who emigrated to Australia but had come into possession of Basil's papers — felt she had not improved the originals by her interventions, perhaps the opposite. The truth is a mystery as the original manuscripts, kept in what is referred to as a 'scrapbook', are lost. It was apparently sent to the National Library of Scotland by Robert, but is not catalogued there now.

Basil Ramsay Anderson witnessed the inevitability of loss and change as a youth, and encoded a brief life's wisdom in this written legacy. It is very good to see that, with this new Northus edition, 'Auld Maunsie's Crü' is once again *ta da fore* and not forgotten, nor is its author and his other work. Anderson deserves to be known more widely, and not only for one masterpiece in Shetland dialect, as I believe this volume demonstrates.

ROBERT ALAN JAMIESON

Edinburgh, April 2021.

Dedicated

BASIL'S MOTHER

AS HE WOULD HAVE WISHED

"The mother's qualities descend, and her influence is felt, through uncounted generations. Thorny may have been her mortal path, many her anxieties and pangs, but if her task has been faithfully accomplished she shall inherit its blessing. In her posterity she enjoys perpetual immortality."

"If the homes the mothers make for the children represent the happy one which lies beyond this earth, if mother and home are what they ought to be, then certainly many a young person will be led by their influence to Father and Heaven."

In Memoriam

BASIL RAMSAY ANDERSON

BORN 6TH AUGUST 1861

DIED 7TH JANUARY 1888

WITH infinite pity and regret, as well as pleasure, I have gathered together such of my young countryman's poems as seemed to speak best for him to his compatriots.

He often brought his verses to me, knowing well that I sympathised warmly in his aspirations, and expected much from his maturer manhood. That such expectations were not ill-grounded may be seen in his writings, from which this volume is a selection. I have used editorial license only in clarifying a passage here and there, or in strengthening a line; and this Basil would have done himself if he had lived to publish any of his own work in book-form.

I make no attempt to describe his life and character here. I have thought that better than any words of mine should be the tribute of those who are best able to judge and speak; and therefore with their permission I quote some of their remarks, merely prefacing those with a few words regarding the "heim-land and heim-folk" from which Basil's Muse was evolved.

He was born in Unst, the most northern—perhaps (its daughter may be pardoned for saying) the most beautiful—of the Shetland Isles. The rush and the roar of nineteenth century civilisation were only then beginning to break on the solitude and voices of Nature which had reigned so long over those isles. The superstitions, the legends, the romance of former days still lingered amid the melancholy moors and lonely valleys; the primitive homes, the rocky *helyers*, the *fiords* and *fiels*. The lives of the peasantry were little changed; and as of old, "the child's lullaby was the hurricane, and his playground the ocean."

Nursed by such influences, a youth of poetic mind was sure to develop into a singer of wild, rugged "*Veeseks*" (Northern ballads); and although Basil Anderson left the Shetland Isles at the early age of fourteen, the surroundings of childhood retained their paramount influence in moulding his character and his Muse.

He was only five years of age when his father was drowned at the haaf (deep-sea fishing).

I remember well the summer squall—sudden, fierce, overwhelming—in which William Isbister's boat went down. He was the skipper, a typical Shetland seaman — handsome, intelligent, energetic, upright. He had a "picked crew," the brothers Anderson being two of these.

Of all the boats which put off from Baltasound, I should have thought Isbister's the last likely to meet with an accident. Yet on that occasion every other boat returned in safety, and none can tell how the ill-fated *sixaerin*, freighted with the precious lives of six good men and true, came by her end. In every case the men left helpless families, and none more so than that of Peter Anderson (Basil's father).

The eldest boy was not more than eight; the only girl was born after the father's death.

How the widow struggled to educate and maintain her six children is known to God, and to few besides. In Basil's touching words to me, "She never grudged us our schooling, but was aye eager that we should never miss a day." Over the hills her little troop used to run, barefooted and but thinly clad, and mayhap after a lighter breakfast than the mother's heart would gladly have bestowed if the "bit at her hand" had been more plentiful. Always neat and clean and eager they came to drink in "schüle-lare," and to carry back to the home, darkened for lack of its breadwinner, the light of intellectual progress.

Her reward has been in seeing her children grow to men—men of whom our Isles may be proud, men to gladden a mother's heart. And though she has also seen the "flower of the flock" gathered, yet she can say, "God kens best what's best for them and me;" and she has Basil's words to comfort her — "Heaven 'ill no' be hame, mither, until I meet you there."

We found among his papers a fragment of song which tells, in simple melodious Shetland words, how tender was the bond between Basil and his mother—

"Na! Na! I widna gie dee yet

For ony lass I see."

And in the same song I find the secret of her influence over him, and his reverence for her—

"Du's ta'en a' dy care ta Christ,

An' I'm ta'en mine ta dee."

(You took all your troubles to Christ,

And I took mine to you.)

A few days before his death, when parting from his youngest brother (parting, as both then knew, for ever in this world), he said, "Ye'll be güde ta Mam" (be tender to our mother).

"Oh, yea! We'll need ta be that," Peter replied; and then Basil whispered, "Güde-bye, then."

Before those last words were said the brothers had prayed and communed together, and that sacred scene will ever remain with the young brother as a most precious and helpful memory.

"Ye'll be güde ta Mam" seems solemnly and sweetly bidding him give her a double portion of love; and in the devotion of this her Benjamin, named after his dead father, the mother will find her chief earthly solace in the days that remain, we shall hope.

Peter says: "Basil was to me, I think, the most beloved of all my brothers: he was very unselfish, large-hearted, childlike in spirit. When a boy he was fiery-tempered … as he grew up he became gentle, and no trace remained of his hot temper. All was subdued and chastened. He was enthusiastic, that was all."

The sister, who came after their father's death, and was the pet of the household, says: "Basil was the life and sunshine of home … He was my nurse and guardian more than the others … Our mother, having to go out to earn a livelihood for us, had to leave me to the care of the boys, and soon this duty fell entirely to Basil, because mother found that nothing ever tempted *him* to leave me alone.

"When I was big enough to go with him, he would take me out to the hill, and show me the wonders of Birdland. He was always a favourite with children, and had a knack of winning their confidence. This was a great help to me, for I was very reserved naturally, but I could always speak out to Basil … The close ties of childhood so formed remind me of his own lines—

'Lay-at a warm side ta a cauld,

And troth ye'll see a towe' (thaw)."

The eldest brother, William, writes of their childhood thus: "I see Basil a little, shy boy with a big head, passionate, energetic nature, clever at everything he tries, dux of his class at school, though always the *smallest* in it, entering into our games with spirit. He could not endure to be beat at anything; and though devoted to his school, he would object to going if he had not learned his lessons in the most thorough manner … At school he excelled in arithmetic and mathematics. Not long before his death I heard him remark that mathematics came easy to him, but Latin was dry, and that he had had to *grind* at it more than at anything else … The only opportunity he had of studying poetry when a boy was from the promiscuous pieces in school reading-books. There was no volume of poetry in our house except a copy of Burns lent us for a time. As we had learned to read in English and converse in Shetland dialect, we could not understand much of Burns … Basil began to compose verses when about twelve. He had a number of pieces in a school exercise-book, which he would read to us; but he would not let strangers see his verses. As he grew up he became very humorous … his religious feelings were very deep, and of an evangelical tendency, yet he sometimes used his humorous faculty with much effect to ridicule old-fashioned or superstitious ideas, in a manner that might shock the extremely orthodox … As I sat by him, not many nights before his death, he said, 'I have always had a hope of getting better, but it is unreasonable to expect that *now*. Somehow I have always felt a natural shrinking from death.' Then after a pause, with a brighter look, he said, 'I have a sure hope now, but my faith (in the past) has fluctuated—sometimes bright and at others cloudy.' "

His brother Robert (nearest to Basil in age and sharing with him in providing for mother and sister) tells me that "thought for his mother was always Basil's first and last idea." He said to Robert as he did to Peter, "Be güde ta Mam."

The brothers were all fond of studying Bird-life, and many happy hours Robert and Basil spent among the cliffs, or on the hills, looking for eggs of wild-fowl, or securing specimens. Robert says that Basil's great aptitude drew the Laird's attention with the result that "he charged himself with a great part of the expenses of Basil's education, etc." This kind-hearted gentleman was rewarded in seeing his protégé win prizes and take first places among his compeers. Robert says "Basil took the senior prize for arithmetic in the Parish School on the 11th February 1873. He was then eleven and a half years old.

"The following spring he was a competitor for the Orkney and Shetland Association's prizes, and passed first-class in the second stage."

"Basil had a very retentive memory. When learning his lessons, everything seemed to come to him with an ease which was astonishing. Arithmetic was his favourite study during his school-days."

Fortunately for Basil his brothers were exceptionally clever, so that he was not "spoilt," as is so often the case with a boy who finds himself "the genius of the family." The wisdom, too, of his mother, while encouraging and fostering all intellectual aspirations, kept in check everything like an over-weening opinion of self — that weed which is planted in naturally modest minds by the injudicious flattery of foolish friends, and which spreads quickly, and chokes many promising flowers of genius.

The Rev. George Steven of Free St. Bernard's Church has given a beautiful and most appreciative contribution to our reminiscences. Having been Basil's pastor makes his words of yet more value.

LETTER FROM THE REV. GEORGE STEVEN

… IT is a pleasure to me to help you in preparing a volume to the memory of our friend Mr. Basil Anderson; and although I have known him for too short a time to speak with any authority, I can at least give you a reminiscence or two.

Let me say at once that there was no young man among us who was more highly respected, I shall say even beloved. Among our young men, he was always "Basil," a kind of brother to every one. Those who knew him best loved him most, and tell many little incidents of his life that bring out his character and affection. At their annual soiree this year a stranger would have been struck with the testimony borne by all the speakers to the worth of the two brothers, and with the expression of most sincere sorrow at their loss.

The first knowledge I had of Basil's poetic gift was at a Band of Hope meeting, where he recited one of his own pieces, which caught me with its playfulness and humour. At the moment I did not know it was his, although everyone else understood. When at last, somewhat later in the evening, they informed me, I have no doubt there crept over me a sense of pride at having a poet among my members. Although he was shy, he was willing to help at such meetings, and those who attended had frequent opportunities of hearing him. There he stood, with his fair complexion and very pale face, reciting rather rapidly, with a very distinct Shetland accent and a cadence just a little monotonous. There was withal a nervous uplifting of the eyebrows, which lent itself now and then to the drollery of his verses. After my discovery, we had many talks about poets and poetry. Of course it was I who introduced the subject, but he entered into it with delight. He listened to me and to my criticisms very modestly, as if he considered me an authority, which made me just a little ashamed of myself, seeing I was none. He told me he had never made a serious study of poetry—indeed had not read very widely in the poets at all. But the books which he knew, he knew well, carried long passages in his memory, and was constantly reading and repeating the best of them. Then again he would tell me how he worked at his verses, and would show me from a printed copy how he was trying by repeated corrections to bring out his meaning clearly. It was touching to think of all this enthusiasm for an art which one was sure he would not practise long. To the end he was but a learner in English, never, so far as I could see, feeling perfectly at ease in it; but in the Shetland dialect he was free, untrammelled. Thus, as the reader will find, his best work was in that; and it is good, direct, strong, living.

Basil was a keen politician, and a great radical, but his radicalism strikes me now as having its source and its strength in a passion of pity for the poor. He had felt the iron in his own life, had seen how cruel the sufferings of poverty might be. And perhaps he did not see what was apparent to us— that it had made him manly: he had learnt in suffering what he was now essaying to teach in song. Occasionally he broke out vehemently against oppression, and now and then there was heard a note of bitter scorn, which was so unlike his general good-temper and charity. What was exceedingly beautiful, and what struck the more thoughtful of his companions was this, that his increasing ill-health never made him in the least sour. With such sensitiveness to the beauty of life, and with a growing knowledge that it would not be his long, there came no bitterness and discontent that things were ordered so; on the contrary, there broke forth a new light. He became subdued, matured, and there died out of him as mere childish ways what little cynicism and hardness had previously existed.

G. S.

*

The English language had been to Basil very much a foreign tongue, and he had found great difficulty in expressing his ideas in it. Thus all his finer poems are in the Shetland dialect. But within the last year or so of his life he had begun to master English in the poetical sense, and make *it* the servant of his Muse. The last time I saw him he recited some of those latest lines, and I noticed a strange pathos in his voice, a weakness of body, a strength of soul, all new. I said (referring to the poems), "That is far and away the best you have written, Basil."

He smiled in a melancholy way which touched me greatly, and answered — lifting himself with a kind of conscious power, also quite new—"I feel as if I had cut the traces now. I write more easily than I did, and I think I shall go ahead faster."

But the fire soon faded from his face, and left what I too surely read was the signet of Death. I bade him good-bye that evening with a premonition that we should not meet on earth again, and that visit was the last he made to any friend.

I have a valued friend less in this world since my young countryman left it.

"What can we say?" writes a brother-poet on this theme; "whom the gods love die young."

I can never look upon the death of a young man of intellect and worth as anything but an unmitigated evil, although orthodox people tell us "it has pleased the Lord" to remove him, and so on.

With all due deference I venture to say it has by no means pleased the Lord—and by "*the* Lord" I mean a good and pitiful Father who willeth not the death of a *sinner,* far less that of one who could have done much to advance His kingdom upon earth.

I prefer to rest in the belief that the Father brings good out of evil, and so makes a promising young life the example, its premature end the warning, to others.

I prefer to hope that the young who pass from earth go to a vaster region, where, untrammelled by the ills to which flesh is heir, their pure spirits find a wider and grander sphere of action. And so I leave "God's will" out of the question. No other comfort can sustain the hearts that mourn for Basil Anderson and his brother Andrew, "both talented, both young, both good, both gone within three months."

*

Basil would wish a remembrance of Andrew to be associated with that of himself, and therefore I shall now quote from the "In Memoriam" sketch which was published at the time of the younger brother's death:—

"Andrew was the fourth son, 'the weakling of our flock,' his brother says. When he was twelve the family left Shetland, but the boy continued his studies, and even when apprenticed and hard at work he continued to find time for much reading and the prosecution of various branches of education.

"When nineteen his health broke down and he was obliged to give up his situation, and with his cousin (son of that uncle who had been drowned with his father) sought the old Island, hoping there to recover their failing strength of body. Poor lads!

"On Andrew's return from Shetland he took classes at the School of Arts and preparatory University classes, and his health rallying somewhat, he became a teacher in a Nautical Academy.

"I am told that he showed wonderful aptitude as a teacher of marine engineers, and that he became quite '*the* man for turning out extra chief engineers.' He had a class in the Leith Science School also, and in both places he gave entire satisfaction, both to superintendents and students. Among these he made many fast friends, for young men and old alike are quick to recognise true goodness when allied to real talent. They recognise it and they honour it.

"That form of consumption which non-scientists name 'Decline' is the bane of young Shetlanders. I do not know whether it is hereditary, or a result of climate, or manner of life; but I do know that it has carried off a number of the fairest and noblest of our country's young men and women. This fatal disease had Andrew Anderson in its hands, and in spite of all his bright hopes, his pure Christian life, his mother's tender care, he faded visibly.

"Last summer he took a voyage to Denmark—the Norseman's cradle—hoping to revive, but returned weaker still, and was soon obliged to give up his classes. Some of his students, reluctant to let the bond fall asunder, came to his house to be instructed, but soon that too had to be relinquished.

"And then the manly young heart prepared itself for the solemn change drawing near.

"He had always been a 'gude bairn,' and had not at that late hour to learn to rest on a Hope beyond earth. Perhaps his dear ones will pardon me if I lift a little corner from the veil which wraps, in their sorrowful remembrance, his last sad and sacred moments.

"'Boys,' he said to his brothers, 'where would I be now but for Jesus?'

"'You'll all come to me in heaven?' At another time—

"'Do not grieve for me.' And so on.

"He bade them all good-bye, saying 'we should meet again,' and like a brave, meek Christian, he yielded his soul to God.

"Tributes of love and respect came from the teachers and students with whom he had been associated, and many of those attended to Warriston Cemetery. In his last days he had bought a share in God's acre for the family, and they laid him there in sure and certain hope."

The fresh flowers placed on that grave in October were lying still unwithered there when they brought his brother to be laid beside Andrew. Basil's spirit was more sanguine and his vitality more strong than Andrew's, therefore it was only at the *very last* that he gave up the hope of life here. But hope in the Life beyond was as firm in him as in his brother; so he gave himself resignedly into his Creator's keeping, and fell on sleep with the trust of a little child, his last words being "Underneath are the everlasting arms."

*

In a brief obituary notice in the *Scotsman* Mr. Gilbert Goudie says of Basil:—

"He early manifested a talent for versification, and had his life been prolonged he would probably have taken a recognised place among our minor poets. His tastes and traditions were all of the North, and to the North his muse, expressed in clever little lyric stanzas in the vernacular of his native isles, was mainly dedicated.

"Shetlanders have complained with reason that, though their country was the land of Skalds and Saga-men, in modern times they have no native poetry, or 'national' songs.

"Burns and the host of Scottish bards are foreigners, whom they barely understand, and certainly cannot appreciate with full sympathy. But of late years a number of native singers have appeared to do away with this reproach by piping lustily, in characteristic notes, the praises of the Isles and their people. One of these was Basil R. Anderson, whose perhaps latest composition was a touching dirge over the bier of another of these singers prematurely cut off: and his countrymen and friends have now to lament his early and sudden loss in the same way. He was of irreproachable character, and much sympathy is felt for his family, who are also mourning the recent loss of his brother."

*

In his own paper the editor of the *Shetland Times* pays a tribute to his young friend:—

"To say that to know Basil Anderson was to love him and esteem him, is as if all were said that written language can express. We recall his first modest communication, submitting some of his early attempts, and requesting a candid opinion as to their fitness. This led to a correspondence which ripened into friendship, which was increased and deepened by our brief—only too brief—personal intercourse during his recent visits 'home,' as he always fondly called it … His constitution was not robust, but his was a brave and cheerful spirit, and underlying the unassuming sweetness and lovableness of his disposition, there was observable a high resolve and noble ambition that augured much for his future … To those who enjoyed the pleasure of his friendship, his name will remain a fragrant memory through all the days to come … To his widowed mother … he was as 'the apple of the eye,' and he returned her love with a tenderness and devotion that was one of his strongest characteristics."

*

In sympathetic language Mr. L. J. Nicolson says:—

"Recollection goes back to five years ago, when a young man sought me out—fair-haired, broad high forehead, large eyes, and pale complexion; and the friendship began that death has now ended. Many a pleasant hour have we spent together, and many a long debate has ushered in the early morning. Pure-minded, open, generous, and earnest withal, keenly alive to the humorous side of life as to the pathetic, his poems and songs were nearly all subjective, the outcome of a broad sympathy with Humanity. The mysteries of life and death had a foremost place in his thoughtful mind … He had the selective instinct in choosing his subjects—fine poetic fancy, and the art to mould his thoughts in melodious verse. Many of his songs accordingly found a musical setting …

We met and walked a little space, and now

I see thee lying in thy lowly rest;

Pale silent lips, closed eyes, and darkened brow;

And I am dumb, for surely it is best.

The flowers are coming forth to welcome spring,

The singing-time of birds is now at hand,

A tender memory to us they bring

For thou art gone into the silent land.

And we shall miss thy voice along the way,

So much less music on our ears will fall;

The great world rushes on from day to day,

One singing-heart is silent—that is all.

The song is hushed that was so well begun,

    To add a name to unfulfilled renown;

And now we come with tears when day is done

    To leave on thy dead brow the poet's crown.

L. J. NICOLSON

*

At a meeting of the Orkney and Shetland Literary Association the chairman referred in feeling terms to the death of their treasurer, Mr. Basil Anderson, and "moved that the Association record their tribute to his memory in the minutes." The secretary, on behalf of the Association, sent a very sympathetic letter to Mrs. Anderson; and she has also received copy of a "Resolution" passed at meeting of the "Free St. Bernard's Sabbath Morning Fellowship Association," from which I quote a few words: "His kind and loving words are vividly remembered by many of the members who now feel that they have lost a warm and sympathetic brother … The life he lived here on earth and the faith he manifested in Jesus Christ gives them the good hope that he has gone to live with Christ which is far better."

*

The *People's Friend* was Basil's friend, and gave him the encouragement that a modest young poet needs. How much the editor can do for the trembling aspirant after literary success is only known to those whose souls have been strengthened by such aid— strengthened to "go in and win." The editor of the *People's Friend* says: "Mr. Anderson had the true poetic fire in his veins … His poetry showed that his tastes were pure and elevating." The same paper publishes a poem by Mr. J. P. Reid, who was Basil's personal friend, and the lines echo of his own Norland muse, therefore I give them here:—

He came from where wild billows gird the coast,

Where sea-foam scuds across the northern main;

Far from the city's busy, hurrying host,

Far from the noise of factory and of train.

And oft we've heard him speak of that "Old Rock,"

 The Northmost of the distant Shetland Isles,

Whose memories he sometimes would unlock,

 And tell its legends o'er with heartsome smiles.

These oft inspired his muse, yet not alone;

 He was a youth of large, broad sympathies,

And tuned his lyre with true and manly tone

 To other subjects different far from these.

Too soon for us his song is hushed for aye!

 The bourne is cross'd, and, free from human strife,

He rests; but brief although it was, let's say,

 The world is surely better for his life!

Basil, farewell! we'll meet on earth no more!

 The Lord hath taken what awhile He gave;

And many a one will sigh in sorrow o'er

 The new-laid turf of thy untimely grave!

J.P. REID

The following acrostic comes from the pen of another of his friends, Mr. J. Rutherford Hill, and may fitly follow Mr. Reid's lines:—

IN MEMORIAM

BASIL—What strangely pleasant memories rise

Around us here in grief, with tear-dimmed eyes,

Seeking a solace for our hearts oppressed,

In some such thoughts as these:—that rest,

Life everlasting and full joy are given

Round that bright throne, to all who dwell in heaven.

And, Basil, thou art there, praising God's boundless love.

No earthly frailty now comes in to stay

Deep fountains of poetic song that pay

Eternal homage as they rise and swell,

Re-echoing praise, and grand in words that tell

Salvation's story—how it was begun

On earth, in thy short life, so quickly run,

Now gloriously complete in that bright home above.

from *Literary Society Magazine.*

Some of Basil's poems appeared in the sixth series of Edwards's *Modern Scottish Poets,* and the editor, quoting from the *Dundee Weekly News,* says of our young singer: "He rhymes with no view to either fame or fortune, but simply to the call of passing fancies that move his imagination when his mind is withdrawn from the sterner duties of life. Like many another he rhymes for his own amusement, and communicates the fact, even to a friend, with almost bated breath, not deeming himself worthy to be reckoned as the least among poets. Every one will appreciate the modesty of this, as it augurs well for the good sense of the possessor of it."

*

Mr. Rutherford Hill, who was intimately associated with Basil in matters connected with Free St. Bernard's Church (of which both were members), speaks of him as "the centre of a great deal" of the church life, and tells me that his early death has made a great impression upon the congregation, who fully appreciated the promising life "cut short at noon."

*

These "tributes" may fitly conclude with the dirge sung by Mr. George Stewart, who was the *first* to rescue (in story-form) our Shetland dialect from becoming lost, and whose graceful and poetic Muse has contributed the sweetest and most characteristic lays to our native poetry:—

THE VOICE OF THULE LAMENTING

AH! weel may sorrow cloud my face
And tears bedim mine eye,
For he wha sweetly sang o' me
Noo low in dust does lie.

l

Like frost-nipp'd flower in early spring
      Afore the sun's bright ray,
The canker struck his feeble root,
      And so he passed away.

Though youngest o' my later Skalds
      (A' humble though they be),
His words best tauld my simple tale,
      Best sang my melody.

Childlike he sat at Nature's feet
      To hear what she would say;
An' as she dropped each gentle word
      He put it in his lay.

An' aye the burden o' his sang,
      Whatever it might be,
Was love o' native hills and dales,
      My bairns a' an' me.

Why, cruel Death, couldst thou sae soon
Deprive me o' a son,
An' tak' him to thy silent land
Ere half his work was done?

Or was his weary spirit faint,
An' dropt its load o' clay
To spread bright wings an' soar awa
To realms o' endless day?

Oh! can it be, unfinished song
He better may renew,
In yonder land in higher strains
Than ever poet knew.

Ye birds that herald in the spring,
Your sweetest notes prolong,
Around the spot where now he sleeps,
Nor heed the passing throng.

lii

But tell the passer-by to let

    You warble aye your strain,

For maist in voice would join wi' you

    Are far across the main.

Ye little flowers bedeck the spot

    Where stands a marble stone,

And clad the sod that wraps the head

    O' Basil Anderson.

GEORGE STEWART

*

In finishing this "labour of love" I would desire to acknowledge gratefully the valuable assistance I have received from sympathetic friends. Mr. Goudie's glossary gives the *Shetland* poems an interest for general readers. He and Mr. George Stewart have given most useful suggestions, and their sympathetic aid has encouraged me greatly. The Rev. George Steven, Mr. J. Rutherford Hill, and Mr. L. J. Nicolson have proved their friendship for Basil by helping with this little volume in many ways.

Miss Lizzie Edmondston has kindly aided in copying and arranging MS., and to Basil's brothers I owe thanks for making smooth for me those portions of editorial work which are often a thankless task.

JESSIE M. E. SAXBY

BROKEN LIGHTS

IN his young manhood Basil stood
      Before the gate of Song;
With eyes upraised, with heart on fire,
With eager fingers on the lyre,
      By Hope upholden long.

And, dreaming, waiting, strove to sing
      Of that sweet hour of rest
When, on the threshold of the night,
The sun-god flings his robes of light
      Ere dying in the west.

Beside that doorway of his hopes,

    At hour of twilight dim,

Our gentle singer heard the call

Of God who frees the soul from thrall

    And gives the harp and hymn.

The Voice divine broke lesser dream;

    It bade him "come up higher,"

And so, with heart assured he went,

And on the threshold dropped content

    His earth-encumbered lyre.

JESSIE M. E. SAXBY

POEMS IN ENGLISH AND SCOTS

NICHT-FA'

THE nicht is gatherin' dark, mither,
      I'm gaun—they ca' it "hame";
But dinna, dinna greet, mither,
      Lest I should Heaven blame.
Ye're aye been dear tae me, mither,
      On earth mair dear than a';
An' heaven will no' be hame, mither,
      Until ye come awa'.

Yet faither will be at the yett,
      He's lippenin' me, I ken;
An' winna it be gran', mither,
      Amang the angels ben?
But nane like me will rin for him,
      They'll a' be far ower braw;
An' aft we'll look for you, mither,
      Oot ower the "jasper wa'."

3

They winna ca' me Johnnie there,

      I'll get a "name" that's "new";

But they'll no gie me wings, mither,

      Lest I flee back tae you;

An' when, tae meet you comin' up,

      I toddle down the hill,

Ye'll kiss me on the mou', mither,

      An' ca' me Johnnie still.

But snugger tuck the claes, mither,

      Yer arms aboot me fauld,

Press, press me closer tae yer breist,

      For, O, I'm gettin' cauld.

Noo lull me wi' a bonnie sang,

      An', mither, dinna greet,

I hear the angels singin', but

      Their sangs are no sae sweet.

A VIGIL

I HURRY home in the darkness,
  The dead mirk fills the sky,
But the lamp still bright in the window,
  Betokens a watchful eye;
Ah, there is no heart like a mother's,
  However that heart we try.

I stand aback on the threshold,
  Ere my heart dare enter in,
Where love sits consecrating
  A sanctuary free from sin.

And the thought comes sharp and sudden,—
  When I shall wandering be
In a night of deeper darkness
  Than falleth on land or sea,
Who will trim a lamp at midnight,
  And keep one watch for me ?

WORK AND SONG

O Maiden! spinning while you sing,
　　And singing while you spin,
Your voice has got a merry ring,
　　Your wheel a merry din;
Long may that happy heart be whole,
　　And never wrung by wrong;
Long may your life be full of soul,
　　Your work be full of song.

The happy birds, because they sing,
　　Line not their nests less soft;
And Commerce spreadeth widest wing
　　When breezes pipe aloft;
Though many a rill with idle dream
　　Comes jingling down the hill,
Full sweetly sings the busy stream
　　That turns the tireless mill.

And poets may have wooed the Muse

      On beds of dull repose,

But what high-priest of song would choose

      The listless lot of those?

The sweetest singer of the West—

      The truest Bard, I trow—

Was truest to himself and best

      When singing at the plough.

THE OLD ROCK

THERE stands an old Rock where the sea-birds flock,
  Afar in the northern sea.
And the wild winds may blow, and the mad currents flow
  Around him in terrible glee,
But he standeth the shock—he's a sturdy old Rock;
And never a rock rocks he!

O proud stands the Rock as the wild waves lock
  Him around with their white clasped hands,
Or kiss his gray feet with their waves rippling fleet,
  And render him tributive sands,
From the glittering cave where the mermaidens lave,
  And the sea-flower in beauty expands;

Then hurrah for the Rock where the sea-birds flock

      Afar in the northern sea:

For the wild winds may blow, and the mad currents flow

      Around him in terrible glee,

But he standeth the shock—he's a sturdy old Rock;

      And never a rock rocks he!

The boast of the Rock was a warrior stock

      In the days when the nations were young.

As Boreas speeds forth from the bergs of the north

      From the Rock of their childhood they sprung.

And a kindlier folk than the race of the Rock

      Never spoke in humanity's tongue:

And still they are brave as their fathers who gave

    Their life-blood so fiercely and free:—

This storm-fostered folk, who are rocked on the Rock

    That rocks not with tempest or sea;

But tosseth on high his proud horns to the sky

    And mocks wind and wave as they flee.

Then hurrah for the Rock where the sea-birds flock

    Afar in the northern sea!

For the wild winds may blow, and the mad currents flow

    Around him in terrible glee;

But he standeth the shock—he's a sturdy old Rock;

    And never a rock rocks he!

HONEST OLÉ

WHERE the angry Boreal breezes
     Sweep round towering Saxa-vord;
And the never weary "woe-drift,"
Driven by the winds like snowdrift,
     Hisseth up the Burra Fjord:

Where Sea-Ha's and haunted Helyers
     Bellow to the wrathful foam;
Where the seagull screams in chorus
With the ocean, wild, sonorous,
     Honest Olé had his home.

Time had rudely told upon him,
     Till like stranded ship he lay:—
Seventy years of deep devotion
Gazing on the face of Ocean
     Might not heedless pass away.

11

Yet he viewed the face familiar

     With that longing look which dwells;

And his eyes would sparkle brightest

When the spumy yeast broke whitest

     Ringing stacks like 'larum bells.

Tho' his bosom-mate still blessed him,

     Flown were parents' pride and worth,—

Stately sons and comely daughters,

Like a wild brood by the waters

     Had been early tempted forth:—

Beckoned and decoyed by Ocean,

     Whom he loved in mirth or war:—

Some to Ocean gladly wedded,

Some in Ocean madly bedded,

     Some by Ocean borne afar!

Still his heart was high and hopeful,

  Till, one night, rode all too free

Up the Fjord the wild, white foam-steed;

And he needs must leave his homestead,

  Tempest-shattered by the sea.

  . . . .

Here the old man's eyes were brimming

  As he told his tale to me.

Well I knew such grief was thorough;

And his saddest say of sorrow

  Was the losing of the sea.

"They have ta'en me from the Ocean

  Calling now with lonely voice.

And I weary for his smiling

For his mad mirth, care-beguiling,

  Bidding this sad heart rejoice.

"Ah! you would not chide my sorrow
        If you knew the loss to me!—
Years of earliest recollection,
Ties of strong and strange connection,—
        All have knit me to the sea!

"Dear ones it has won and wafted
        In its moods of mirth and war!
Some to Ocean gladly wedded,
Some in Ocean madly bedded,
        Some by Ocean borne afar!"

        .   .   .   .

Now he sleeps beside the Ocean,
        And his last words come to me,
Fraught with frenzy in their measure,—
"When the Sea gives back its treasure,
        They will give me back the Sea."

COME, GATHER THE WEALTH OF THE WAVE

COME, gather the wealth of the wave, with a will—

    'Tis sin that the harvest be small;

We've only to reap where we never can till,

    And there is abundance for all.

We never have tilled, but we ever must toil—

    Success only waiteth the brave;

Yet, poor, we may gather a surfeit of spoil

    By robbing the rich teeming wave.

    Then gather the wealth of the wave,

    Come, gather the wealth of the wave—

    By the death of the fishes that swim in the sea

    The life of the people we save.

Come, gather the wealth of the wave—lend a hand
    To eke out the dole of supply;
Nor fear that the ocean shall fail, till demand
    A glutted and stagnant pool lie.
God giveth few gifts to the beggar who stands
    Stucco-stiff like a statue all day,
But bestoweth on him who beseecheth with hands,
    And bendeth his body to pray.

    Then gather the wealth of the wave,
    Come, gather the wealth of the wave;
    By the death of the fishes that swim in the sea
    The life of the people we save.

Come, gather the wealth of the wave—it is free—

Thank God! 'tis not bound like the land!—

The length, and the breadth, and the depth of the sea

He holds in His own hollowed hand.

Where thousands are starving there need not be one,

If only we list to the call;

But the harvest will pass, and the summer be done,

And God is the judge of us all.

Then gather the wealth of the wave,

Come, gather the wealth of the wave;

By the death of the fishes that swim in the sea

The life of the people we save.

"DEATH TO THE HEAD THAT WEARS NO HAIR"

This is an old Shetland Toast. It sounds grim and deadly enough, until one realizes that it merely means death to the hairless fish!   J. M. E. S.

FILL up, fill up the burnished cup,

    The Holland gin's divine, Sir!

Drain every drop before you stop,

    'Tis better far than wine, Sir.

Drink deep, and fast, and do not spare—

"Death to the head that wears no hair,

    And strength to hale the line, Sir."

Another draught, and when 'tis quaffed

    We yet will have another,

This one goes down the last to drown,

    The next one this to smother.

Drink deep and fast, 'twill banish care—

"Death to the head that wears no hair,

    And life to every other!"

So "Health be thine, and health be mine,"
      This pledge we aye will quaff, Sir,
For honest health at crazy wealth
      May well afford to laugh, Sir.
Drink deep and fast, the nectar rare—
"Death to the head that wears no hair,
      And glory to the haaf, Sir."

The crowning glass, and we must pass—
      Such moments last not ever,
The one we meet and fondly greet,
      The next again we sever.
The tide invites, the breeze is fair—
"Death to the head that wears no hair,
      And good luck leave us never!"

TWILIGHT

WHEN the Sun-god's fiery chariot
      Has attained the glowing west,
Wide are flung the golden portals—
Wondrous sight to eager mortals—
      To receive him to his rest.

Short he pauseth on the threshold
      Ere retiring for the night;
Then the great gates close behind him,
Leaving, of their bars which bind him,
      Crimson streaks of parting light.

Ere descend the wings of darkness
      To envelop all in gloom
Comes the quiet silver Twilight
Heralding, to earth and sky, Night,
      Blushing like a rose in bloom.

Soft the sighing west wind whispers

    Words of love among the trees;

While the wailing of the plover,

Like a sad desponding lover,

    Plaintive answers to the breeze.

Mirthful music makes the streamlet

    As it babbles down the glade

Thro' the mead and tangled wild-wood—

Happy as the days of childhood

    With its blue sky overhead.

Fitful songs come from the branches

    Whcre the birds have gone to rest,

Homeward then a far-strayed bee flits,

But each flower with folded leaflets

    Hides its honey in its breast.

Rapt I gaze in adoration

    Of the beauties all around,

And I, pensive musing, ponder

As I ever onward wander

    On their teachings, high, profound.

O what lessons read we in them!

    To the wounded here is balm:—

Tho' ye see your day declining

Cease from fevered Day's repining,

    Twilight brings a holy calm.

Sweating labour, faint and weary,

    Sinks into the arms of rest.

Hushed are fretting care and sorrow,

Hope portrays a glad to-morrow,

    Grief in silence veils her crest.

So, when Life's soft twilight fadeth,

Let not tear-drops, cloud the eye.

Why should we be broken-hearted?

'Tis the light of the departed

Sun that gilds the evening sky.

Thus the lamp of good men shineth

When their sun sinks in the west;

And their thoughts and actions guide us,

As if *they* were still beside us

In this world of wild unrest.

Ne'er shall fade their hallowed radiance

Till the Christian's morn arise:

And their souls, more bright and glorious,—

O'er the night of Death victorious

Shall return to glad our eyes.

THE HERRING KING

Ho! heralded high by the sea-mew's scream,

King Herring has woke from his winter dream,

   And royally rides in his glory forth,

While wide are the wings that are spread for the north.

O there's flesh on the land, and there's fish in the sea,

But the herring is king, and only he!

Then here's to the bluff-bowed boat that rides

'Neath the silent stars on the swelling tides,

   To follow the flash of his silver sides,

    And hunt the herring king!

With a wag of his head, with a toss of his tail,

He beckons the bark with the dark-brown sail;

And who, like a sluggard, would slumber and sleep

When the herring king rides on the crest of the deep?

O nursed on the breast of the northern sea,

  The herring is king, and only he!

To hands that are willing, to hearts that are bold,

He casteth his scales in silver and gold,

And standeth a friend in the moment of need,

The naked to clothe, and the hungry to feed.

O blest be the homes that look to the sea,

  For the herring is king, and only he!

O eyes! that have gazed for the loves you lack,

Till your far-away look never more may come back;

Sisters and sweethearts! mothers and wives!

If the herring king giveth, he taketh lives.

O the song and the dirge of the northern sea

Is—the herring is king, and only he!

Then here's to the bluff-bowed boat that rides

'Neath the silent stars on the swelling tides,

    To follow the flash of his silver sides

    And hunt the herring king!

THE FURTHER HAAF

SWEETLY smiled the morning,—a new-made bride aglow—

    Glad arose the glorious sun,—a bridegroom he—

Six sturdy oars flashed in the waters of the Voe

    And six brave hearts put out to sea.

        "O, the sixaerin's aff

        To the far, far haaf!

        God guard our ain," sang she.

Dull grew the mid-day sky with dark clouds bending low,

    Wild screamed the bold sea-gull, a storm-sprite he,

White flashed the foam-caps on the waters of the Voe,

    And sad came the moan of the sea.

        "O, the sixaerins aff

        At the far, far haaf!

        God save our ain," sighed she.

Wild rose the midnight waters, madder yet their flow.

Strong hearts were stilled amid that tempest's glee.

And hungry eyes long long shall gaze beyond the Voe,

And hearts shall break as breaks the sea.

For the sixaerin's aff

To a far farther haaf,

God help thy bairns and thee.

THE MARINER'S DEATH

FOR the salt foam he left his home
> To earn his loved one's bread;
The angry wave became his grave,—
> He had no narrow bed.

No coffined plank was where he sank;
> The sea-bird screamed his knell;
No darling near to shed a tear,
> Or bid a last farewell.

But on the gale the mermaid's wail
> Rose weirdlike on the storm;
While ocean wild and undefiled
> Enwrapped his lifeless form.

Though in the deep he went to sleep
> Lulled by the wandering wave,
As calm his rest beneath its crest
> As in an earthen grave.

I SIGH FOR THE ISLES

I SIGH for the Isles that are over the sea,

I sigh for the hearts of the North;

For I know that a welcome is waiting for me,

And I know what that welcome is worth.

I have basked in the smile of the stranger awhile,

      Though the stranger is courteous but cold,

And I'm longing to-night for the light of a smile

      That is richer than guineas of gold

      Richer than guineas of gold,

    Treasure of measure untold,

I am longing to-night for the light of a smile

      That is richer than guineas of gold.

I know there are hearts in the world around

Beating tender and true as can be,

And for every pearl of price that is found

There are scores in the depths of the sea:

Yet I sigh for the land that is over the sea,

      The isles of the uttermost main;

And I dream of fond hearts that are dreaming of me,

      And I long for a presence again

      Long for a presence again,—

      Soothing and smoothing all pain ;

I dream of fond hearts that are dreaming of me

      And I long for a presence again.

MAGNIE'S AWA'

O MAGNIE'S awa',
The blithest o' a',
Like a flower turned ower i' the furrow:
His fiddle nae mair
Will banish oor care
Or lichten oor hearts when we sorrow.

A' covered wi' dust
Untouched noo it must
(Tae think o't my heart is nigh breakin')
Hang dumb on the wa':
For there's nane ava
Like Magnie its notes can awaken.

The lasses will miss

The moments o' bliss

They kent when its shrill tones were screechin',

An' sigh i' their heart

For Magnie's blithe art

They loved spite the minister's preachin'.

But tho' he is laid

In his low, narrow bed

An' the green grass is springin' above him,

His name shall remain

A tender refrain

In the hearts of the lasses who love him.

A FOUR-YEAR-OLD

A little cousin who preceded the author to the "Better Land."   J. M. E. S.

HE'S a bright one, I can tell you,
> Tho' he's but a four-year-old;
Merry eyes and cheeks of dimples,
Where a stream of laughter wimples,
> All-controlling, uncontrolled.

Cherry lips of rosy ripeness,
> That his lovers all adore;
Sunny hair and brow of brightness;
Chubby hands that lose their whiteness
> On the dusty kitchen floor.

See him doting like a deaf-mute—
> Heedless, silent, pensive—till
Bang! he wakes with romp and rattle,
Storming all with brawl and brattle,
> Like a sluice set on a mill!

34

Daily thus he buildeth castles

On the floor and in the air;

Daily thus they prove unstable

As Alnaskar's in the fable,

Built and shattered with his ware.

O, the little elfin angel,

How he makes his mother rail!

Turns the house into a Babel,

Overthrowing chairs and table,

Crawling after pussy's tail!

Many a scratch on face and fingers,

Dealt by puss in furious wars,

Will he show you, gladly, proudly,

Talking of them long and loudly,

Like a soldier of his scars.

Well, he is a little soldier;

    You would laugh to see him drill—

How his gun he smartly shoulders,

To the mirth of the beholders,

    As he stalks the floor at will!

Now he turns upon you fiercely,

    Points with deadly aim his gun,

Cries "tum-tum," and charges on you;

While, to show that he has won you,

    You must either fall or run.

Bible tale and fairy legend,

    In confusion reckless flung,

Interspersed with rhyming clatter—

Secular and sacred matter—

    Rattle from his tireless tongue.

"O his tongue wags," say his sisters,

      "Worse than all the city bells"—

Never was there known his fellow;

All their sweethearts he will tell you—

      Mina's, Jessie's, Betty's, Nell's.

Yet they pet the little rascal,

      Give him kisses, sweets, and toys;

Till, it strikes me, if I gather

Rightly, such fair martyrs rather

      Like these ways of little boys.

And whene'er, at ebb of daylight,

      Father's footfall wakes the stair,

Off he eager bounds to meet him,

Pouting all the way to greet him

      With such sweet lip-laden ware.

And soon by the blazing bright hearth,

    Striding the paternal knee,

Rides he fast, and fast, and faster—

Tireless as a tyrant master,

    Who delights in cruelty.

While, in cross-examination,

    Father can but scratch his head

At the queer and curious questions,

Gravely linked with naïve suggestions,

    How the riddles might be read.

What the sun, moon, stars are made of;

    Whence they come and whither go—

Goes the sun to bed at even?

And are stars just lamps in heaven,

    Lit like other lamps below?

But when night's more dusky curtains

      Fully close around the skies,

Gently slumber seals his eyelids,

As the angels seal the sky-lids,

      And the dreamy stars arise.

God protect him, little darling!

      Hearts and hopes and home to fill;

Oft our loving arms enfold him,

And although at times we scold him,

      Well he knows we love him still.

THE OLD MAN

(TO MY GRANDFATHER)

HOW I love to see the old man
      Sitting by the blazing fire!
When the nights grow darker, colder,
Winter winds wax wilder, bolder,
      And the fitful flames leap higher.

Planted in his favourite corner,
      Snug shored in his elbow chair,
Like a hero in his glory,
Giving forth some quaint, queer story,
      As his pipe-fumes cloud the air.

Who such yarns could spin and weave you—
      Warp and woof, you marvel how—
As this old romantic sailor,
And, to boot, bold Arctic whaler,
      Though his hulk is shattered now!

Pictures of the wondrous old time,

     Painted by a master-hand!

Scenes, sublime, burlesque, and tragic,

Lit with fancy's rays of magic,

     Glorious, grotesque, and grand!

How the children gather round him!

     Eyes, and ears, and mouth as well,

All attention, eager drinking,

While the little mind is thinking,

     And the soul is bound by spell.

Thus from first to last, untiring,

     Follow eyes with wild unrest;

As some flowerets, ever gazing

Sunward, while that orb is blazing,

     Mark his course from east to west.

And as glances of the sunbeams,

    Falling on cold winter's brow,

Make his frozen face to glisten;

So their glances, as they listen,

    Wake the sage's smile e'en now.

Till the pride of days departed

    Fires anew the old man's breast;

As the glory, erst of morning,

Evening's deepening, dark shades scorning,

    Floods the bosom of the west.

Now, the wondrous tales suspended,

    Off to bed the children go;

While the old man's memory lingers,

As he spreads his frozen fingers,

    To the kind, congenial glow.

On the long-lost friends of childhood,

      Youth, and manhood, riper still;

And bright Fancy's pencil traces—

Portraits?—nay, the living faces;

      Firebrands conjuring at will.

But his brow grows sad and thoughtful

      As the spent fire sinketh low;

And, far in his soul's hid chambers,

As he poreth o'er the embers,

      Spectral shadows come and go.

Visions happy, like the fire-light,

      Faded with each fated brand,

Twofold darkness mantles o'er him;

But the hero looks before him

      To that brighter, better land.

Hush! his spirit is transported!
      'Tis no vision dark and dim—
In his heaven-lit visage read it—
Darkness reigns; he doth not heed it,
      For it is not night to him.

Mar not sweet anticipation
      Of re-union with the dead;
Leave him, leave him softly sleeping,
Bright the star-dreams vigil keeping—
      Angels hover o'er his head.

THE ISLES OF THE NORD

(A SONG OF HJALTLAND)

O SING me no sorrowful home-sick song,

Of the land of the Voe and the Vord;

For my heart is as light, and my arm is as strong,

As they were in the Isles of the Nord!

And the Norseman of old was a warrior bold,

Ever tempted to far lands by danger;

And still in my creed his precept I read,

That the Norseman is nowhere a stranger.

Then glad be the song, as in days when the wrong

Was righted by might of the sword;

When the battle raged long, and the Norseman was strong

Who came from the Isles of the Nord.

Yet sing me a home-breathing, heart-stirring song,

That shall thrill me with deepest accord;

For the Norseman, though freely afar dwelling long,

Aye remembered the Isles of the Nord;

And the spoils of the war, that were gathered afar,

Where the Norseman was never a craven,

Came back to the land of the conquering brand,

'Neath the guardian wing of the raven.

Then proud be the song, as in days when the wrong

Was righted by might of the sword;

When the battle raged long, and the Norse-man was strong

Who came from the Isles of the Nord.

O sing me a song, I shall cherish as long

As this bosom one throb can afford;

And the land of my love be the land of your song,

The heart-stirring Isles of the Nord;

For the Norseman of old made the Isles his strong-hold,

In the days when he first was a ranger;

And the dear, rugged strand of the far rocky land

Still inspires him 'mid daring and danger.

Then high be the song, as in days when the wrong

Was righted by might of the sword;

When the battle raged long, and the Norseman was strong

Who came from the Isles of the Nord.

UPWARD

O THE valley of life is pleasant,
  Where sweetly the pilgrim may rest;
But his must be toil incessant
  Who would climb to the eagle's nest.
There is love in the poet's valley,
  There is fame on his dizzy height;
But my head is giddily swimming,
  And I cannot dare the fight.

A few lion-hearted as Browning
  Have clambered to carve them a name,
While love-looks like glory are crowning
  Less heroes with chaplets of fame.
But my brain like a madman's is fiery,
  And racked by a terrible strain,
And he that would rifle the eyrie
  Must not loiter to lilt in the plain.

Yet lend me your love, gentle daughters

      Of sires who were victors of yore,

And bathe my hot brow in the waters

      Of your kind-flowing pity once more.

And pledge me a bowl that is brimming,

      And hardships and dangers I'll brook;

For heroes are born of women,

      And fate is a woman's look.

SHETLAND HOSPITALITY

AWAKE, my muse, thy simple strains
To sing, 'tis surely worth thy pains,
When such a theme the soul enchains
    As Shetland hospitality.
The clouds shall stay for aye their rain,
The waters deep forsake the main,
The burning sun grow pale, and wane,
    Ere it grow cold formality.

Tho' scant and poor the soil may be,
Hard won the harvest of the sea,
The Northman's hearth and board are free
    To grant beyond equality.
Tho' small his unimposing hut
Nor night nor day the door is shut,
The stranger "ben," the "kinder" "but"
    Is Shetland hospitality.

Thou who can'st every prayer fulfil,

With blessing load, protect from ill,

And grant him, if it be Thy will,

    To whet his hospitality,

A blazing fire, a steaming kiln,

A gushing flood, a whirling mill,

Nor stint his ocean harvest still

    In quantity or quality.

TO A LERWICK LASS

ON RECEIVING PHOTOGRAPHS OF SHETLAND SCENERY

DEAR Mary, since that morning bright
    Thy kindness smiled on me,
I've had it in my inmost heart
    To sing a song to thee.

I feel a presence here to-night,
    I grasp a proferred hand,
And, prophet-like, I seem to view
    Mine own dear Northern land.

And of the many Northern Lights,
    Whose glory track the sea,
It is the brightest paves to-night
    The silvery path for me.

’Mong happy scenes of sea and shore
        Once more I roam at will—
By towering cliff, by ancient "brough,"
        By merry water-mill.

Dear Unst, my own, my well beloved!
        O fairest isle to me
Of all the many bosom-gems
        That stud the Northern Sea!

With joy I hug thy rugged sides,
        Where high-crowned Saxavord
Looks down on Muckle Flugga Light
        And swelling Burra Fjord.

Where Sumburgh lifts his horned head
  To hold his lantern high,
I stand and listen to the waves
  That wildly hurry by.

With awe I view the deep abyss
  Where Noss's cradle swung,
And deem that here when ocean wakes
  His wildest songs are sung.

By Mousa's Pictish brough I roam,
  A thoughtless truant child,
Unknown to care as bird of air,
  And glad in nature wild;

By Scalloway's historic pile,

      I ponder long and deep,

Like digger that disturbs the dust

      Of centuries asleep.

But ever and anon I feel

      That soft hand leading me,

Where Lerwick, like a fair maid, dips

      Her bare feet in the sea.

I had a song—forgive, sweet maid,

      These babblings of the tongue—

Still, still within my inmost heart,

      My song remains unsung.

THE DARKENED LAMP

It was an old belief in the Isles that when some dear one, at a distance, was dying, the Lamp at home wore a "broch" (misty halo) and its light waned at times. This poem was written a few years ago in memory of a young Shetlander who died in Australia, and to whom Basil was much attached. "Gripsy" was his dog.   J. M. E. S.

PART I

ERECT in the first flush of manhood,

    In vigour of arm and of brow,

He had flinched not from duty nor danger—

    He had flinched not, and could not flinch now.

Thus he stood in that little home circle,—

    Thinned sorely already, God wot—

The heart and the hope of a household,

    The soul of one sweet little spot.

Thus he stood, and a sure voice came calling,

    One night in the gloaming so gray,

Like a far-dwelling trumpet that signals

    To fain hearts that wait for the fray.

Prophetic he heard it, and heeded
　　As a soldier who buckles for war;
(We know that it came from afar off,
　　But we knew not it came from *so* far).

Our hearts sorrow-melted and aching,
　　Saw a strange mystic light in his eyes,—
He bade us good-bye, and we blessed him,—
　　Face set for the far sunny skies.

So over the ocean he vanished;
　　But always our hearts thought of him,
As a strange silence fell in the gloaming,
　　And the lamp wore a misty-like rim.

How often we wondered and blamed it!
　　How often the wick we would trim!
Ah! we would not have blamed it so often
　　Had we known it was misty for him!

PART II

Yet again came the voice, clearer, nearer,
    In that bright, sunny land far away,
Distinct as a trumpet that calleth
    Tried hearts to a yet farther fray.

Prophetic he heard it, and heeded
    As a soldier all buckled for war;
And over a yet wider ocean
    He followed, and set like a star.

Now the hush of the gloaming is deeper,
    And all things are deader, I know;
E'en the old clock that made such a ticking,
    Wag-waggeth so silent and slow.

Our wishes, our wants, and communings,

    In a speech that is voiceless we tell,

For a silence that cannot be broken

    Has come in our household to dwell.

But whenever poor Gripsy uppricketh

    Those sharp ears so trusty of yore,

O! blankly our eyes meet each other,

    Then tremulous turn to the door.

And as last he stood there on the threshold,

    Through a haze we again see him stand,

And our hearts fill with longing to follow

    Away to that far, farther land.

Then the lamp burneth dimmer and dimmer,

    Till darkness creeps over its rim,

But we blame it not *now*, as it wavers,

    For we know it was darkened for him.

A CRY FROM THE POOR

O IS there a God in the Heavens?

    Or has He been drowned in the sea?

Or feedeth He only the ravens

    Who feast on the feeble with glee?

No; He hath appointed Him stewards

    To deal out the gifts of His hand;

But faithless are all but a few hearts,

    And fettered with foibles the land.

The earth is the Lord's and its fulness,

    The land, as the wave and its wealth;

Deem ye, silly dolts, in your dulness,

    That stealing from God is not stealth.

Your calves feed and fatten on riches,

    While hunger is gnawing God's poor;

Your statues have canopied niches,

    While human heads houseless endure.

No flint-heart is Earth in fruitions,

    No niggard of riches or room;

Yet hardship is lord of conditions,

    To huddle hordes into the tomb.

Requires not the Hand retribution

    That fully and freely bestowed?

Declares not the law substitution—

    "Who giveth the poor, giveth God?"

Come down from your temples of splendour

    To Misery's squalid ravines—

More cursed the bright guilt of your grandeur

    Than all the dark guilt of these scenes.

Stretch the hand to your brethren who languish

    In slums for the sake of a crust,

And own in the hell of high anguish

    How sadly you've failed in your trust.

But a muffled cheer breaks from the masses,

    Like the breath of a Samson unbound,

As, thro' clenched teeth, the hissed whisper passes

    "Too long in the prison we've ground."

Then remember, ye brothers of Abel,

    As ye bring of the fruit of the ground,

God's altar is Poverty's table—

    Take care it be worthily crowned.

NIGHT

WHO is this Night, dim-lighted, and arrayed
     In softest shadowy mantle, rustling sweet
Among the leaves, as down the wooded glade
     She gently glides—while, babbling at her feet,
The merry brooklet bounds with glee along,
As if to win her smile with willing song?

Hark! the low moaning of her stricken breast
     Finds fitful echo in the cushat's croon,
While eagerly she reaches to the west,
     As if her hope had sunk there—and too soon!
Say, canst thou gaze upon that shadowed face,
Nor know those features, one of shining grace?

O widowed Day! I knew thy early morn—

      Thy smile was sweet, thy carol sweeter still—

When, toying with the golden-headed corn,

      'Twas thine to lightly bound o'er vale and hill,

Despising Time, who robbed thee as he flew,

Yet seemed to clothe thee in a beauty new.

Thy noontide's splendour—evening's setting calm—

      I knew their happy hours, and loved them all;

And, when the throstle trolled his farewell psalm,

      I marked thy sun—how glorious his fall!

And saw thee widowed, don thy weeds of woe,

And thought thee fairer than in noon's full flow.

O how I loved thy melancholy grace,

      As, sitting by thy lost hope's lonely bier,

 'Twas thine to fold across a shadowed face

      The hands that hid the softly stealing tear;

While yet shone forth that majesty of mien

Which, even in thy sorrow, crowned thee queen.

And now the stars in sympathy arise,

     Their melting lustre gleaming on thy gloom—
No vain consolers they, whose heavy eyes

     Would cheer the bride by weeping the lost groom,
But beautiful and bright, O Night, like him
For whom thy lamp is burning low and dim.

Thy balmy kiss is soothing to the soul,

     Thy cooling breath is pleasant to the brow,
Thy silent dew-tear consecrates the whole,

     There never was a lovelier than thou.
Clasped in thy dear embrace of darkness deep
The weary find repose in dreamless sleep.

But I delight to linger in thy shade,

     And pour my musings in thy patient ear,
With thy star-spangled banner overhead,

     And whispering night-winds banishing all fear.
Let others pant for fame and court the light,
I am content unknown—a child of Night.

CLOUD AND STAR

'Twas in the golden days of childhood's mirth,
  Within our home beside the raging main,
When sitting by the blazing cottage-hearth,
  Wild fancies flitting weirdly round my brain,
I watched the spark and curling smoke ascend
  Towards the liquid blue ethereal sky,
And thought, in sweet simplicity of mind,
  Sparks made the stars, and smoke the clouds on high.

These childish thoughts have set, but, like the sun,
  They left their traces on life's varied skies;
So that I do not like to count them gone,
  But often dwell upon their memories,
And live again ideas long gone by;
  For truths as deep as Science's self can tell
(Concealed, it may be, from the careless eye)
  Within their depths in happy wedlock dwell.

Say, does not man, the heaven o'er his head

    Cloud or bestud, by doings dark and bright?

Good acts are like the starry sparks, bespread

    Upon a firmament of spangled light.

And from the vapours of Life-clouds arise

    The bootless aim, the act devoid of good—

For such no brilliant stars shall ope their eyes;

    His welkin shall be dark and leaden hued.

NIGHT THOUGHTS

THE night has sunk. The deeper blue
The glad-eyed skies are looking thro',
To draw our hearts to Heaven anew.

Our Father's love in all we see,—
The leaf that falleth from the tree
Must change, but not be lost; and we?

We will not fear till shattered fall
The blue round of the larger ball,
The high dome of our Father's hall.

We hope, we trust, we are sufficed.
The stars and angels keep their tryst:
We go to fall asleep in Christ.

THE BUSY STREET

TO-DAY I was wrapt in musing,

     As I passed by the busy way,

And I could not refrain from choosing

     The theme of this simple lay.

O! that some lots were less hard,

     Or that I could sing a song

To lighten the loads that press hard,

     On hearts that must hurry along!

       With breaking beat!

       With breaking beat!

O God of love! can it be meet?

And never a sigh from the busy street!

What surging of forms and faces!

What spinning and speeding of wheels!

What sweating of flanks in traces!

What flashing of hoofs and heels!

What hard-headed struggling and striving!

What trampling of many by few!

What random and reckless driving!

What terrible grand review!

The busy street!

The busy street!

In rattle of wheels and hurry of feet,

Throbs the mad pulse of the busy street!

Like the surge of the swirling waters—

    Wave ever with wave at war—

Its voice by the sons and the daughters

    Is eagerly heard afar:

And the fairest hope of the village,

    And the flower of the mountain side,

The coils of its maelstrom pillage

    To sink or to swim in its tide!

      The busy street!

      The busy street!

Tho' Fame may beckon and Fortune greet,

What brave hearts sink in the busy street!

'Tis said that we all are brothers;

    That a "common lot" we share;

That our joys and our woes are each other's,

    And the mutual load all should bear;

Yet human hearts yield not pity,

    Tho' pity moved Horeb's hard rock;

And there break, in the heart of a city,

    Hearts ne'er in the desert had broke!

      The busy street!

      The busy street!

Where thousands meet and never greet,

How lone and cold is the busy street!

O high hearts of freedom and lightness!

And heavy hearts, muffled and sad!

Brows beaming with beauty and lightness!

Brows bent, with the dark shadow clad!

Eyes lighted with love and with goodness,

Thro' which we may gaze to the heart!

Eyes burning with lust and with lewdness,

That charm but to strike with a dart!

And busy street!

O busy street!

How fall off the fair, the pure, the sweet,

Soul-stained with the soil of the busy street?

Yet the street has a glow and a gladness
      Of its own for the kindred heart,
Who can drown all sorrow and sadness
      In the rush of a busy mart;
And pulses of passion and pleasure,
      That throb with a wilder beat
Than the furious madcap measure,
      Trod by its flying feet!
         But I hate the street!
         I hate the street!
And I long to be where the wild waves beat
With a purer pulse than that of the street!

LICHTSOME HEART

DEAR frien's, in wanderin' on thro' life
    Whatever be your part,
Thro' joy an' sorrow, calm an' strife,
    Aye bear a lichtsome heart.

When showers o' happiness doonpoor
    Ne'er think upo' life's ills:
Such thoughts will only mar the hour
    And cup that pleasure fills.

Aye look upo' the brightest side,
    And ye will ne'er gae wrang;
Tho' cauld adversity betide,
    Gie't welcome wi' a sang.

Think when ye stand on trouble's brink
    Amid the gathering gloom,
A heavy heart will gar you sink,
    A licht will mak' ye soom.

Rack na your brain wi' anxious care
    Nor fret your life away;
But if your load's too hard to bear,
    Let it row doon the brae.

An' seek yersel' a lichter pack
    That winna weigh ye doon;
Man wisna made to brak' his back
    Nor yet to crack his croon.

Dear frien's, in wanderin' on thro' life,
    Whatever be your part,
Thro' joy an' sorrow, calm an' strife,
    Aye bear a lichtsome heart.

SUNSET

I STOOD as day departed
      And twilight dim came creeping,
Too sad and heavy-hearted
      To vent my woe in weeping.

With slow step night was stealing
      Far over dell and down,
While curfew's notes came pealing
      From yonder neighbouring town.

I sighed for dying daylight,
      By western waters sinking;
And in the dusky, gray light
      I sat alone bethinking.

The dreary shadows wandered

    In heavy tracks behind,

As back my thoughts meandered

    'Mid spectres of the mind.

'Mid all the glowing fancies

    Of youth's bright early dream,

That vanished like the gladness

    Of Sol's retiring beam.

But memory of gone faces

    Still lingered in my mind,

As in the west bright traces

    Of day delayed behind.

I thought of that fair morning

    When night shall pass away,

And, all the world adorning,

    Shall come the endless Day.

Then, like refreshing moisture,

    There fell a soothing balm;

And never sure in cloister

    Was felt a holier calm.

The heavy cloud of sadness

    Was lifted from my soul,

And a new glorious gladness

    My spirit did enroll.

NIGHT SHADES

THE sombre shades of evening
      With parting beams of light
Come drifting through the gloaming
      As birds flock home at night:
Come sailing slowly, slowly,
      Sweet shades of Paradise;
They hide Day with their plumage
      To show their vigil eyes.

The sombre shades of evening
      Come clouding o'er my soul,
That wakes with wintry moanings
      And thoughts that darkly roll:
For though the stars look through them
      With lustre-beaming eyes,
My troubled spirit wavers
      Below those troubled skies.

O soul that shrinks in sadness,

    O soul that grieves 'mid gloom!

Find in those shades of evening

    Good angels of the tomb.

They come to close in kindness

    A failing life's dim eyes,

And bear the sun of life-light

    To never-shadowed skies.

ALONE

GO, let me vent my tears alone,
      That free their tide may flow;
My heart is like the smitten stone
      When Moses struck the blow,—
'Tis heavier far than any stone,
      And gushing o'er with woe;
For there was one where now is none,
      And none my grief may know.

The troubled fountains of the deep—
      The fountains of my grief—
Burst from the silence of their sleep
      To sob forth their relief:
As waters waked from wintry sleep
      Break every barrier reef;
But they who weep shall surely reap
      One day a golden sheaf.

A golden sheaf!—O God! O God!

      Cold comes the black, black night.

Yet Day shall lift that dreary load

      Upon his wings of light:

As cold as night our shrouded load

      Lies very stark and white,

But what lies trod below the sod

      Returns no more to sight.

Ah! they whose loved are lost do know

      What 'tis to be alone;

And pitying tears but idly flow,

      As waters lap a stone:

Like snails within their shells who know

      No presence but their own,

Deep warped in woe we darkling go

      Alone, alone, alone!

"GOD IS OUR DEFENCE"

SONG OF THE SECOND E.R.V. CORPS (MOTTO OF CORPS)

TRAMP, tramp, tramp, tramp, we come, we come
     A gallant proud array—
A phalanx marshalled to the drum
     And martial music's lay.
The fire of daring lights each eye
     In all the column dense;
Our patriotic veins swell high,
     And "God is our defence."
          Then let the might be with the right,
          Hence, bloody tyrants, hence;
          Our arm is strong to spurn the wrong,
          For "God is our defence."

Tramp, tramp, tramp, tramp, we boldly march

    With firm and measured tread,

The blue of heaven's ethereal arch

    Triumphal o'er our head.

    Sworn foes to shackled slavery,

    We stand, a free-willed fence,

Around the shrine of liberty;

    Yet bound in this one sense.

        Then let the might be with the right,

        Hence, bloody tyrants, hence;

        Our arm is strong to spurn the wrong,

        For "God is our defence."

Tramp, tramp, tramp, tramp, our aim is peace,

 Tho' war may be our theme,

Till bitter strife and carnage cease

 To swell the tyrant's dream.

Nor court we bloody, bootless wars

 On any vain pretence;

But be it known we're sons of Mars,

 And "God is our defence."

  Then let the might be with the right,

  Hence, bloody tyrants, hence;

  Our arm is strong to spurn the wrong,

  For "God is our defence."

THE BOOK

THE Bible of our fathers,
      Deep dyed in Scottish gore,
Now sleeps upon the Peace-shelf
      Dust-clad an inch and more;
Or, one day out of seven,
      When priestly hand unhasps,
Lolls on a tasselled cushion,
      With all its golden clasps.

But once, its home the moorlands,
      Its couch some rocky ledge,
It glittered on the inside,
      And not upon the edge,
And, dressed in simple sheep-skin,
      Inspired our Parent-stock,
While gilt and polished goat-skin
      Now better sway the flock.

THE NORTH WIND

I LOVE, I love the North Wind,
>> That brings the white-robed snow;
The boreal, boisterous, free wind
>> Bold Winter bids to blow.
Now, shrieking in weird gladness,
>> It wildly, madly raves;
And now, in sighing sadness,
>> Moans to the surging waves.

So proud it sweeps from Northland,
>> So dauntless hurries past,
As if the souls of sea-kings
>> Were riding on the blast;
While comes its untamed music
>> With reckless rise and fall,
Like some loud wassail-chorus
>> From Odin's festive hall.

Rejoice, then, son of Hialtland,

    When Boreas rideth forth;—

The spirit of thy fathers

    Comes rushing from the North;

Defiant still it sweepeth

    O'er ravaged sea and shore,

Unconquered and all-conquering,

    As in the days of yore.

And as it ploughs the ocean,

    It ploughs my ravished soul,

Till, thrilled with deep emotion,

    And roused beyond control,

Like storm-stirred clamorous sea-mew,

    My spirit answers high,

And pours to winds and waters

    Her wildest minstrelsy.

TRUTH

DIGGING for Truth in the heart of the earth,
  Great is the labour like searching for gold,—
  Slow is the process like searching for gold.
Rock and rubbish embedding its worth,—
  Truth, Truth they closely enfold.

Seeking the pearl of greatest price,
  Diving for Truth in the unfathomed seas,
  Sifting for Truth the sands of the seas;
Shells of glitter and gilt despise,—
  Truth, Truth dwells not in these.

Searching for Truth in the heavens above,
  Scanning the orbs of the midnight skies,
  Seeking the loadstar of Truth in the skies;
Try not its virtue by planets that rove—
  Truth, Truth judge not by lies.

Battling for Truth from morn till eve,

      Never relinquish till life-light is done,—

      Never give in till the conquest is won;

Prove all things by Truth before you believe,

      And Truth, Truth will shine like the sun.

THE MERMAID'S SONG

A MERMAID sat on a rock by the shore,

    A-combing her hair with a red coral comb,

As a mariner, bending him quick to the oar,

    Came sweeping along o'er the foam.

Her ringlets of gold waving bright in the breeze,

    Her bosom of snow heaving gladly the while,

She wantonly sang a weird song of the seas,

    The heart of a stone might beguile.

Old ocean e'en silenced his billowy roar,

    And hushed his proud wave while the mermaiden sung;

And the mariner rested him then on his oar

    To list the wild sea-notes that rung.

"O fair are the halls of the broad briny deep,

    Resplendent the wealth of their glittering sheen,

And many earth-heroes do peacefully sleep

    Where none but the mermaid hath been.

"The sun's burning rays may not pierce thro' the waves,

    Not far down below may his yellow light creep;

But gems rare and living enlighten the caves,

    And shine in the cells of the deep.

The wealth of the mountains can never compare

    With the Treasure untold and unheeded that lies

Where the daughters of ocean bewitchingly fair

    Allure by the light of their eyes.

"There flowers of the ocean in beauty do bloom,

    And gracefully lift their sweet faces on high,

Or willow-like bend o'er some famed hero's tomb

    Where mermaidens pause oft to sigh.

What tho' not a leaf of the laurel or bay

    Begraceth the brow of the sea-buried dead,

He lies amid coral, and many a spray

    Of sea-weed enwreathes him instead.

"The land has grown changed, and gloomy, and drear,
    But, fair as creation's hand left them at first,
The beauties of ocean all changeless appear,—
    'Tis only the earth that's been curst.
O fair are the halls of the broad, briny deep,
    Resplendent the wealth of their glittering sheen,
And many earth-heroes do peacefully sleep
    Where none but the mermaid hath been."

The song died away, while awakened the breeze,
    And ocean rolled on with his slow-measured sound,
But the mariner dream-like reclining at ease,
    Knew not that his soul was spell-bound,
O who could a voice so melodious and sweet
    Not touch with its tones till it charmed him to rest?
The mariner's spirit the music did greet
    As notes from the land of the blest.

The sea-maiden plunged in the breast of the wave

    That wreathed her white bosom in glistening foam,

Her fair flowing tresses the billow did lave,

    And loosed from their red coral comb.

And fast o'er the ocean she merrily sped,

    While glided the mariner's barklet behind,—

Tho' oar was not handled, nor white sail bespread,

    Its speed yet out-rivalled the wind.

And never again did that sailor return

    To her whom he loved, and who wept for his doom,

Until her lone spirit no longer could mourn,

    And she sank to the cold silent tomb:

But oft-times when lowering and dark grows the sky,

    Is seen on the face of the waters a light,

And a bark, with the wings of the wind, rushes by,

    Led on by a form shining bright.

And weird notes are heard to arise on the gale,

   Enchanting and sweet as a soft-sighing lute,

That soothing, as oil on the waters, prevail

   Till tempest and billow are mute:—

"O fair are the halls of the broad, briny deep,

   Resplendent the wealth of their glittering sheen,

And many earth-heroes do peacefully sleep

   Where none but the mermaid hath been."

AN ANGEL OF THE NETHER BLUE

HER eye betrayed the briny tear;
>Her glistening locks, the briny foam;
And piteous were her sobs to hear;
But, hushing doubt and soothing fear,
>He led her gently home.

Tho' wintry winds in wrath had rung
>The welkin wide with furious glee,
Till rebel waves had heavy swung
With wreck and weed, and outcast flung
>A daughter of the sea.

O fairer far than maids of earth,
>Sweet angel of the Nether Blue!
Would she not grace a Norseman's hearth
Above all ranks of wealth or birth?
>And love would follow too.

He drew her from her doubts and fears;
  He won her love, at least in part;
He saw her smiling, tho' thro' tears,
And vowed to love her thro' the years;
  And heart replied to heart.

She bore to him a noble stock,
  A dozen fair-haired boys and girls:
But oft she sought the lonely rock,
Where first her ocean-dream was broke,
  And sighing combed her curls.

O was it that her husband's bark
  Rode far the angry treacherous foam,
She thus would wait from dawn till dark,
The restless wave to watch and hark,
  Till dear hearts forced her home?

Or was she tempted to the shore
        By long-pent yearnings to be free,
And still within her bosom bore
The sad responsive heart of yore,
        Concentred in the sea?

Ah, who might tell? Time swiftly flew—
        Too soon her fair and comely flock
To man's estate and woman's grew,
And, wild-winged as the white sea-mew,
        Forsook their native rock.

Then sad she wandered by the shore,
        As one who longeth to be free;
Her speech grew strange as mystic lore;
She only spoke for evermore
        The language of the sea.

And once when storms assailed his bark,

A pale, sweet face, too well he knew,

The Norseman 'mid the surf did mark,

And sighed that home and life were dark,

As shoreward fast he flew.

His brow ne'er lost the sorrow-dew,

No more he ploughed the salt-sea foam,

But daily scanned with mistful view

The Higher and the Nether Blue

As doubtful of her home.

AN OLD SONG

O SING again that song to me,
    And I will list it o'er;
Its sweet and soothing melodie
    I fain would hear once more;
For I to-night am sorrowful
    As ne'er I've been before;
And nought can soothe a troubled soul
    Like the sweet songs of yore.
    Then sing again that song to me,
        And I will list it o'er;
    Its sweet and soothing melodie
        I fain would hear once more.

It lulled my babyhood to sleep

     Upon a rock-bound shore,

And now, like music of the deep,

     It thrills me to the core—

It breathes like odours from the sea,

     That winds to faint heart bore;

And brings with it the memorie

     Of the dear days of yore.

     Then sing again that song to me,

       And I will list it o'er;

     Its sweet and soothing melodie

       I fain would hear once more.

The voices of departed friends,

    That whisper now no more,

The sighing of the plaintive winds,

    Old ocean's measured roar,

Come back across the tide of Time

    To banish sadder lore,

And cheer as bells, at Christmas, chime

    The happy peals of yore.

    Then sing again that song to me,

        And I will list it o'er;

    Its sweet and soothing melodie

        I fain would hear once more.

OLD AND NEW

THE new moon came out yesternight,

　　　Nor alone, for the old moon came too

And the children went mad with delight

　　　To see them hug high in the blue;—

　　　　　How they crew

　　　At the old in the lap of the new!

They dragged forth the dog and the cat,

　　　And tugged at their grandfather too;

But the old man just smiled where he sat,

　　　And, bending him low, got a view

　　　　　Of the two

　　　Thro' the pane they so sweetly shone thro'.

But sad were the thoughts they awoke—

    The thoughts and the memories too—

For never a word now he spoke

    And dimmer his dim eyes grew

        With a dew,

    Nor his coat-sleeves their sight could renew.

Ah, children! the thoughtless and gay—

    The happy and innocent too—

Light-hearted as merles in May,

    When you lift up your bright eyes of blue

        If you knew

    What truth-telling mischief they do!

Though old lights may outlive their day,

    And, fondly we cherish them, too,

They are shadows of moons passed away,

    And we must look up to the new,

        As the true,

    To lead us to dare and to do.

TWO BUDS

I GAVE my love a budding rose,
      One cloudless morn of early June,
My ardent passion to disclose,
        Her heart with mine to tune.

I watched the blush upon her cheek
      Grow deeper than the rose's hue,
And read what words could never speak
        In eyes of living blue.

Tho' soon, thought I, its bloom shall fade,
      And haply, like the rose-bud, too,
My love-bud in her breast lie dead,
        Incense outliveth hue.

Then die the flower of equal date,
      Altho' I grieve my love-bud's doom,
I'll even glory in its fate—
        Embalmed in such a tomb!

A LOVER'S DREAM

I DREAMT I was a summer breeze
That, sighing, murmured thro' the trees,
Then spied a rose, and wooed a rose,
And eased my soul of all its woes.

I dreamt I was a solar ray
Shot from the sky at peep of day,
And lighting on a wreath of snow
Made it to melt in genial glow.

I dreamt I was a pale moonbeam,
And struggling forth I kissed the stream
That with sweet murmur gave consent
As over it I fondly bent.

I dreamt I was the noontide sun,
My love a dew-drop to be won,
So, strong with fervent heat I grew,
And to myself the darling drew.

A TRUE MAN

HE was but a poor man
      The wealthy had scorned,
Yet never a truer man
      Minstrelsy mourned.
His failings were many,
      For flesh will be weak,
But who hath not any,
      Let him blaming speak?

Tho' seldom seen praying
      And never to preach,
His life, aye essaying,
      Great lessons did teach.
He bore like a hero
      The cross for the crown,
Yet suffered no Nero
      To trample him down.

He envied not any

> Though wealth might be theirs,

He asked not the many

> To carry his cares.

Yet happy, contented,

> And peaceful he dwelt,

And died he lamented

> With sorrow heartfelt.

RECOGNITION

WE passed each other on the street,
  But, ah! why was it so,
We could not let our glances meet,
  But thought of long ago?
Both had affected memory dead,
  Yet could not don the lie,—
And so she blushing hung her head,
  And flurried I passed by.
    The flowers that with the summer fade
      Renew their bloom with May;
    And can the love I've held as dead
      Be green again to-day?

She droop'd not lily-pale and lorn;

    Her cheek was yet as red,

Nor wore her lip the curling scorn

    That sneers at passion dead.

I only saw the maid I loved

    When all was bright below;

And do you marvel, sirs, it moved

    My life-tide's fuller flow?

    The flowers that with the summer fade

        Renew their bloom with May;

    And can the love I've held as dead

        Be green again to-day?

We met, but as the many meet

    Who pass each other by:

And yet that meeting on the street

    Brought dimness to mine eye.

O was it passion waked anew

    That tender mist I shed?

Or was it but the fitting dew

    That memory gives the dead?

    The flowers that with the summer fade

        Renew their bloom in May;

    But never more the love that's dead

        Resumes its virgin sway.

A FAREWELL

WITH eyes tear-dimmed and sorrow-rimmed,
    Bold son of Song, we give the grasp
With clinging clench that feels the wrench
    Even as our knitted fingers clasp.

Farewell! the hardest word of all,—
    Not that we would not wish thee well;
But thro' the soul's mysterious hall
    Its echoes vibrate like a knell.

When fall the shadows of the night,
    And quiet musings fill the breast,
We'll think of one who, like the light,
    Has passed into the far, far west.

And thro' the vista of the years
    Will smile the bow of hope unriven;
As, shining through the earliest tears,
    At first to fallen man was given.

A HIDDEN GEM

LINES FOR A YOUNG LADY'S ALBUM

(Read first letter of first line, second letter of second line, third of third, etc.)

METHOUGHT I stood beside a silver sea,

Gazing into its limpid depths, where lay,

Rare in their beauty and their brilliancy,

The gems of fairest dye and purest ray.

So plunging headlong to secure a prize

A casket was my meed, wherein there lay

The fairest pearl that ever tempted eyes;

And, that it lead not simpler hearts astray,

The casket here I close and warning give,

My riddle read not, if in peace thou'dst live.

The following three poems I found in a very fragmentary condition among Basil's papers. The sentiments were so excellent that I have "trimmed" them as I think he meant to do, and added them to his other verse.

J. M. E. S.

A BONNIE FACE

I'M fairly ower the lugs in love—
    But that's nae sin ava;
The lass I loe is far abune
    A' ithers I e'er saw.

There's something in a bonnie face,
    Though beauty be its a',
That makes a man forget a' grace,
    An' steals his heart awa'.

There may be little sign o' wit,—
    There may be nane ava!
But I can thole the want o' it
    If beauty be her fa'!

And when the lass has sense an' grace,

     Is guid as well as braw;

O wha wad blame the bonnie face

     That stole the heart awa'?

THE SPELL OF THE SEA

SWEET child from a far rocky Isle,
     With eyes of the deepest of blue,
I give thee a tear and a smile,
     The soul's melting sunshine and dew.
For, but with a look, thy young heart unto me
Brought the spell and the myst'ry of the North Sea.

I felt thy sad soul touching mine,—
     Too thoughtless I asked of thy name;
For answer those eyes, so divine,
     And accents betelling "Auld hame,"
Said, "the dear name *he* bore—O ask not of me,
'Tis hid evermore in the fathomless sea."

I knew then what magic had bound

 So closely thy heart to my heart:—

The loved who in ocean are drowned

 Knit lives that are widely apart.

For earth's highest brotherhoods, strong tho' they be,

Cannot bind like the great orphanhood of the sea.

O sad and mysterious Deep,

 What ties have been broke by thy swell!

O ye who 'mid wild waters sleep,

 Our hearts own your love-hallowed spell!

O child ever dear, ever nameless to me,

'Twas God linked our souls by the chain of the sea.

PRESENT YET PAST

("I think this refers to our grandfather."—W. J. A.)

I'VE sung on many a homely theme
  While this has waited long:
Has it been insult to the dead?
  I now redeem the wrong.
But ah! the silent tide of grief
  Has gathered fast and strong,
Ere such deep channel of the heart
  O'erflowed in sorrow-song.

I miss his kindly reverend face,
  I miss him everywhere,—
And yet his omnipresence seems
  To float upon the air.
But vain I stretch my eager arms
  Towards his vacant chair,
For where his shadow haunteth most
  He is most absent there.

He sat beside our quiet hearth
      When winter winds blew wild,
And brighter kindled up the blaze
      When he caressed the child.
Now gone the gladness and the grace
      That every grief beguiled,
And Darkness spreads its dreary wings
      Where once the old man smiled.

POEMS IN THE SHETLAND
DIALECT

FRAGMENT

ADDRESSED TO HIS MOTHER

O' A' da sangs I'm ever sung
      I'm never sung o' dee
Tho' a' da sang *du* ever sang
      Wis "Hushie ba' " ta me.

Du's hed de mony a weary oor
      Sin' first du cradled me,
But du's taen a' dy care ta Christ,
      An' I'm taen mine ta dee.

Sae let me tak de roond da neck
      An' look deep i' dy ee:—
Na! Na! I widna gie dee yet
      For ony lass I see.

AULD MAUNSIE'S CRÜ

PART I

OOT-OWER upon a weel-kent hill,

Whase watters rise ta grind a mill,

Auld Maunsie biggit him a crü,

Ta growe him kail for mutton brü,—

For Maunsie never thocht him hale

Withoot sheeps' shanks an' cogs o' kail.

Noo Maunsie's wis as guid a tongue

As ever psalm o' Dauvid sung.

It fittit weel a godly mooth,

An' said few wirds 'at wirna truth,

An' never swore by Guid or Deil

Excep' whan kyunnens ate his kail.

Maunsie never muckle fashed wi' schule,

Aye wroucht by random mair than rule;

But, drew he plan or drew he no,

He set the steead an honest O;

An' sune da neebors roond a' saw

Rise up a stanch sheep-hadden wa';

While, laek a man inspired wi' hope

He clappit on da hindmost cope,

An' as he sew da seed an' süt,

Wi' touchts o' kail he schowed da cüt!

Auld Maunsie's crü was fair ta see,

A tooer an' landmark ta da ee.

Whan Nickie soucht da fardest haaf

He pointed wi' da huggy-staff,

"Noo Erty keep her ta da Nord,

Tak Maunsies crü on Byre o' Scord."

An' whan a schooner took da soond

Let ance her head be heilded roond

Deil oucht da skipper hed ta dü

Bit had her for Auld Maunsie's crü.

Mair noted far dan clock or schime

Auld Maunsie's crü proclaimed da time:

Just as the sun raise ower da crü

Auld Lowrie o' da Liogue raise tü.

Whan ower da crü da sun wis high

Oot staagin' cam da Setter kye:—

What had na folk ta truck an' dü

Afore he heilded aff da crü!

Fae Gaapaslap ta Swartagerts

Da crü was kent dat mony erts

Dere wis nae oor in a' da twall

But in some place some tongue wid yall

Ta langsome legs an' elbucks tü—

"Da sun is by Auld Maunsie's crü!"

Whan Betty Bunt 'at bedd in Virse

Wis riskin reeds an' gorsty-girse,

Auld Maunsie's crü below the sun

Said "Hame an' see da denner on."

Noo, if her limmer o' a lass

Ne'er heedin' hoo da time wid pass

Sat purlin' wi' her lazy taes

Among da ase, afore da aze,

Shü'd stamp, wi' sic an angry fit,

"What! no' a tautie washen yet?"

An' swear sic oaths baith sma' an' grit

As weel micht mak a crü ta flit.

"Hing on da kettle i' da crook

Or, troth, I'll flatten laek a fluke

Dy sweery carcage whaur du sits.

Gude fegs! du'll pit me by me wits!

Da sorrow scad dee in his brü—

Da sun is by Auld Maunsie's crü!"

An' whan at last da sun gaed doon,

An', bricht an' bonnie, raise da mune,

Auld Elder Rasmie o' da mill

Grew restless as shü neared da hill,

Gaed twa'r-tree casts aboot da floor,

Dan, solemn, soucht again da door,

But never crossed his smuck da goit,—

Just nose an' nicht-kep gae a scoit,

For süre as I'm a sinner tü

Da mune wis heildin aff da crü!

So stappin inby i' da neuk

He haarled oot da muckle Beuk,

Spread wide his naepkin ower his knees

Ta keep da holy brods fae grease,

Lickit his toom ta turn da laef,

Said "Lord, da baess hae got der shaef.

We leuk ta Dee, laek aalie sheep,

Ta gie wis schowins frae da Deep."

Da schapter read he bowed him doon

An' prayed 'at He wha rules abüne

His haund roond dem an deirs wid keep—

For He wid wauk tho' dey süd sleep—

An' gaird der herts laek stocks o' kail

Fae dat black kyunnen ca'd da Deil.

An' staund a wa' aroond dem tü

Far sürer dan Auld Maunsie's crü.

PART II

Whan winter skies gae ne'er a flame

An' lads were linkin' oot "fae-hame,"

Or whan da mists lay ower da hill

Till raikin' dogs wid even will,

Auld Maunsie's crü, set on da heicht,

Wid tell da rodd ta left or richt,

An' when da snaw was driftin' deep

Da crü was soucht by cruggin' sheep,

Whaur safe an' snug dey'd buried lie

Till fanns wir scoomed, or drifts wir by.

Whan simmer tuik cauld winter's place

An' a' da hills wir run wi' baess,

Here mares, an' foals, an' pellat rüls

Wid come at nicht ta mak der büls,

An' wheygs an' calves wi' "moo" an' "mü"

Wid bless Auld Maunsie for his crü.

At last, despite baith sheep an' kail,

Maunse an' his crü began ta fail.

Time booed his rigg, an' shüre his tap,

An' laid his crü in mony a slap,

Snug-shorded by his ain hert-stane

He lost his senses ene by ene,

Till lyin' helpless, laek a paet,

Nor kail, nor mutton he could aet;

So dee'd, as what we a' maun dü,

Hae we, or hae we no', a crü.

An', strange ta tell, da nicht he dee'd

His crü, in raabin' ta da steead

Laid stiff an' stark his yearald rül,

A' mangled in a bluidy bül:

An' sae da corbie, an' da craw,

'At flapt der wings ower Maunsie's wa',

Wi' mony a "corp" an' "caw" did say

A sowl wis flit fae aert dat day.

Dan aff on roosty wings agein

Ta hook da ro an' tear his een.

But years gaed by as aye de'r geen,—

Da winter white, da simmer green,—

Da voars aye sawn, da hairsts aye shorn,

Aye some ane dead, aye some ane born:

Auld Maunsie's name an' fame wir spent

But still his crü-steead wis aert-kent.

But, less! its name troo time wis lost:—

Folk aye wir fey ta raise a ghost;

So after bein' named by a'

"Da crü o' him 'at's noo awa' "

(Lord rest his sowl!) it cam ta geng

By da füle name o' "Ferry-ring."

An' so wi' age an' moss grown gray

It waddered mony a heavy day,

But o' da wa's 'at ance wir seen,

Da mark an' guide ta mony e'en,

Deil stane wis left but ane or twa

Upstaundin' whaur hill-baess could claw.

An' later folk had mair ta dü

Dan mind Auld Maunsie or his crü.

IRONBONNS, DA MAN O' MICHT

DER cam a craetur fae da Sooth

Wi' glowerin' een an' gapin' mooth:

Gude faith! I weel may say da laek

O' him wis never kent ta spaek!

He read intil auld skin-cled beuks—

Blue-finned an' aeten roond da neuks;—

For days, in kirkyards, never shiftin'

He lay laek some puir baste in liftin';

He scoored troo mires an' moory lochs,

He rade clean daft ower auld Pechts brochs;

Wroucht weeks on weeks, wi' wheer mill-picks

By auld crü-steeads, an' raubit deks;

An' ranged an' raikit a' da hills

For vod geese-skyaags, an' watter-mills.

He'd read in some auld Norne sang—

Wi' sic a name an' sic a twang—

(No' wrate in ony year o' Guid,

But fifty year afore da flüd.)

O' some strange shooskie o' a king,

Wha's whillie brook on Swarta-taing

Upon her staarn wis painted bricht,

Name, "Ironbonns, da Man o' Micht."

So when his body cam ashore

Below auld Tammy Turrell's door,

Dey took him ower across da hill,

Awa' by Olé's watter-mill,

An' dere dey planted Ironbonns,

An' ringed him in wi' mossy stonns

Ta keep his grave fae dicklin' yowes,

An' sain his body fae da Trows.

Ae day wir craetur, in a fix,

No' kennin' whaur tae try his picks,

Yet oxterin' a muckle pock

Ta hadd da bruck 'at he micht hock,

Guid troagin' oot-a-daeks until,

Bewilt wi' mist i' ta da hill,

He staagit lost, when—or he kens,

He stumbles ower a ring o' stanes

An' swarfs awa'; but, by my sang!

He beddna fae his senses lang—

Den swöre an' blessed da Pooers at anes

For tumblin' him ower Ironbanes.

He made a pit, an' hockit deep—

As Andrew kent 'at lost his sheep—

An' wan by wan dey cam ta licht

Da iron bones o' Him o' Micht!

An' deeper yet he sank an' sank,

An' still da bonns cam ta da bank;

Tho' aye wi' every idder chunt

He wharried up an auld kail-runt.

Sae wroucht he, till da nicht cam doon,

Wi' nedder sign o' star or moon.

Dan grovellin' for his empty pock

He stuffed her wi' da muildy stock,

Fulfilled Ambition's highest drēm,

An' wi' da lede guid laeborin' hame.

Wir Wautie met him i' da mirk

Gyaun staagin' by da muckle kirk,

An' as he stottit ower da stonns

Wis heard da clank o' Ironbonns.

Wi' inward glee, an' ootward groint,

Bonn till his bonn, an' joint ta joint,

Steel-rimmed an' bund wi' strong bress-wup,

He bade auld Ironbonns staand up!

An' shiverin' in his naked bonns,

Weel-shorded ta da knees wi' stonns,

Ance mair da famous Man o' Micht

Stüde up ta shaw da world his heicht.

News güid laek wild-fire troo da Isle,

An' folk cam troagin' mony a mile:—

For south ta Sumburgh, nort ta Scaw,

Deil ane his fellow ever saw.

STROOPIE I' DA ASE

"THE MARCH OF THULE"

I'M bulgit in shape laek a widden Dutch cap,

Wi' a haand oot behint laek a hump on my back,

A nicht-kep abüne, wi' a hole i' da tap,

An' my craig stentin' oot till ye'd tink he wid crack,

Sittin' laigh i' da ase wi' a taand at my tail,

Yet I sing laek da steamer whin in wi' da mail!

I ance wis as sheenin' as new-blecket shüne,

An' smit a' da bairns wi' madram an' glee

Whin I shawed dem deir faces as broad as da müne;

Yet noo, when dey're bodies, dey're madder for me,

Tho' black as da baak, yet I'm bricht ta da aald,

For I keep up deir hert, an' dey keep me fae caald.

O da happiest sicht I can wiss man on aert,

(An' da prayer o' my hert is "Guid sicht may he see!"),

Is da brünnie-spread ribs in a üle by da hert,

An' a blazin' fire huggit wi' pussy an' me,—

He at da tae sheek, an' I at da tidder,

Singin' in chorus laek sister an' bridder!

I warm up da hert, yet I fire na da bluid;

An' weel can I wash doon a bere-burstin' crül;

An' sud ye want sometin' ta dü you some guid

At voar-time, at hairst-time, or even at Yule,

At castin' da paets, or at biggin' da dess,

Commend me ta Stroopie 'at sits i' da ase!

For tho' bulgit in shape laek a widden Dutch cap,

Wi' a haand oot behint laek a hump on my back,

A nicht-kep abüne wi' a hole i' da tap,

An' my craig stentin' oot till ye'd tink he wid crack,

Sittin' laigh i' da ase wi' a taand at my tail,

Yet I sing laek da steamer whin in wi' da mail!

COMIN' FAE DA HILL

"SO Betty! ye're been wast da brig

     For twa blue clods to raise a lowe?

Lord grant ye mayna brak yer rigg;

     For, troth, I tink a hedder-cowe

Wid noo be freight enough for you,

Why did ye rin yer keshie fu'?

"Ye'd be da better o' a staff,

     Ta keep yer feet gaen up da brae.

So Gude be wi' you; I'll be aff—

     I'm gaen ta strick some teck da day.

But neist time 'at ye want twa clods

Just try wir hame stack—what's da odds?

"Lamb, I'll just carry what I can;

But blissins be in every bane,

An' mak dee, jewel! a stately man

For dy sweet kindness—so, du's gane.

Da Lord len' me his heevinly staff,

Till Christ sall lift my keshie aff."

FRAM

"WEEL, Betty! better day we couldna wiss;

    So, wi' yer büdie ye'll be troagin' fram?"

"Lamb, dat am I; bit whatna ting is dis?

    My! sic a bonnie jewel lost its mam."

"Yea: sorrow lay auld Maunsie in a stank;

Wir moorit yowe is smored i' his nort bank.

"An' peerie Johnie's iggit me a' voar

    Ta bring him hame a aalie-lamb come simmer—

What will he? tank da Lord 'at gaarsed her smore

    An' sent him sic a mooty ting o' gimmer.

Heth, if I'd only lat my twa haunds lowse

Dey'd buggy-flay some carcage by da yowe's.

"Bit whan'll ye be wir wy neist? Dey say

It's maist a cüre for sair een noo ta see you:

For it's been fram wi' you dis mony a day.

Bit blissins, lamb." "O blissins, blissins wi' you,

Less! I'm a weary wastral wanderin' fram.

Lord, caa me hame Dy ain Christ's aalie-lamb."

HEIM-FOLK

O SOME say da fram an' da frem'd ir da best,—

Da fram may be fair, an' da frem'd may be free,

Bit I laek da heim-land abune a' da rest,

An' I laek da heim-folk 'at bide by da sea.

   For heim-folk are kind folk,

   An' heim-folk can mind folk,

Ta welcome dem back wi' a hert ever free;

   Tho' heim-folk be few folk,

   Yet heim-folk are true folk,—

O Güde spüre da heim-folk 'at bide by da sea!

Tho' heim-herts laek sea-birds, a far-fleein' flock—

Ta a' erts are scattered on every breath;

Da kindest, laek lempits, still stick ta da Rock—

O late be da ebb when dey'r pickit by Death.

        For heim-herts ir near herts,

        An' heim-herts ir dear herts,

Commend me ta heim-herts wharever dey be!

        Yet still dey'r da nearest,

        An' still dey'r da dearest,—

Güde spüre dem!—da kruipins 'at bide by da sea.

DA RESTIN' O' DA FIRE

DA auld wife sat her spinnie at,

  Till shü did fairly tire;

Da auld man gude, da kye ta feed,

  Fu' sax times i' da byre,

An' aye cam' in an' hinted syne,

  'Twas time ta rest da fire;

Yet, tho' sae late, ta tak' da gaet

  Da lad shew nae desire.

For, plantit snug beside da lug,

  Da rogue ne'er seemed ta tire—

He wisna blate ta sit sae late,

  An' brook an elder's ire;

While Merran sat wi' kindly chat,

  An' plied her busy wire:

Dey windered what da lass wis at,

  Shü widna rest da fire.

Da auld man said "It's time for bed,"

    Yet gude intil da byre;

Da auld wife took paets oot da neuk

    An' laid afore da fire;

Yet still shü sat, tho' ill, I wat,

    Sin' Mirren did defy 'er:

It saired her richt dat weary nicht

    (De hag! shü ne'er was higher!)

But aff ta bed at last shü gude,

    She couldna spin for aye:

Nor could the auld man be sae bauld,

    Again ta feed da kye.

Sae flytin' wild, da twa, beguiled

    By slumber, did retire;

While lass an' lad, despite dem mad,

    Sat up ta rest da fire.

THE LADDIE HE WAS BLATE

THE laddie he was blate,

An' the nicht was wearin' late,

An' what could a puir lassie do, do, do?

Her heart was throbbin' sore,

For a rappin' at the door

Tauld anither lad was wantin' in tae woo, woo, woo.

She lo'ed the laddie weel,

For in her lap, atweel,

A lot o' unco ferlies he let drap, drap, drap;

But it lookit sae absurd

That he never said a word,

And aye there came the ither laddie's rap, rap, rap.

Noo the lad was gyaun awa'

Far a towmont, maybe twa,

An' she micht never see his face agen-gen-gen

Sae wi' a heart fu' sore

She saw him tae the door,

An' the ither laddie bauldly steppit ben, ben, ben.

He crackit blythe an' croose,

Seemed sae hamelike i' the hoose,

An' syne frae aff his finger drew a ring, ring, ring;

What could the lassie do,

Tho' anither she did lo'e,

When it slippit ower her finger, puir thing, thing, thing.

The weddin' day was set,

An' the weddin' farles het

Were just waitin' to be eaten, or tae cule, cule, cule,

When the postman gae a rap,

An' the word flew in her lap

That her ither lad was comin' hame gin Yule, Yule, Yule.

The lassie noo took ill,

An' far an' far'er still

The bridal day, sae blythesome, was put aff, aff, aff,

Till 'twas feared by a' the toon,

She wad need nae weddin' goon,

But a white windin' sheet in her graff, graff, graff.

But hoo the lassies blinkit,

An' the chaps on ither winkit,

An' the auld wives hotch'd an' leuch wi' a ha, ha, ha!

When her first love cam' back,

An' the lassie took the tack

Like a ship that wins the weather, though it blaw, blaw, blaw.

Noo shes got anither ring,

Yet the kind-hearted thing,

Lest the jilted laddie dee wi' the dool, dool, dool,

Tae return his ring is laith,

Sae she's wearin' them baith,

An' we'll a' shak' a leg gin Yule, Yule, Yule.

THE SNELL WINDS ARE BLAWIN'

A FIRESIDE SANG

THE snell winds are blawin' baith eerie an' glum
    But cosie an' crouse we're the nicht;
Though Boreas, the bogle, may rair i' the lum,
  Big bairns are kittle tae fricht.
The glamour that glints i' the glowe o' the peat
  Enlivens an' sweetens the smile,
Sae hirsle yer chairs in a circle complete,
  An' glower on the glorious pile.
      Then circle wi' story, wi' sang, an' wi' joke,
            The lowe an' the glowe o' the fire;
      An' the spunkies will keek thro' the curl o' the reek,
            An' winkin' an' lauchin' expire.

Pyromancy nae wizard it taks ta unfauld—

  The heart o' a hame is the hearth,

An' love is but unco whaur heartstanes are cauld,

  An' love is the heaven o' earth.

The blink may be bauld i' the Black Chiel's howe;

  But e'en i' the heaven abune

They hae a bit spunkie tae gie them a lowe,

  When the darg o' the day is dune.

    Then circle wi' story, wi' sang, an' wi' joke,

      The lowe an' the glowe o' the fire;

    An' the spunkies will keek thro' the curl o' the reek,

      An' winkin' an' lauchin' expire.

Like Judah o' auld, 'neath his vine or his fig,

  May we sit 'neath oor ain riggin'-tree,

While plenty an' peace wi' the gray sparrows bigg,

  An' bide though the gay sparrows flee.

An' lang may the lowe loup that scares frae the hearth

  The darkness, like murky-winged craws;

An' ne'er may the kin or the fremmit see dearth,

  Wha picture wi' shadows oor wa's.

     Then circle wi' story, wi' sang, an' wi' joke,

          The lowe an' the glowe o' the fire;

     An' the spunkies will keek thro' the curl o' the reek,

          An' winkin' an' lauchin' expire.

LIVIN' COLLS AN' CAULD CLODS

IN comes peerie Johnnie wi' his fingers frozen taws,

Oot upo' da toonmals he's been rowin' snawy baas,

"O dünna lay da cauld clods up ta da lowin' taands,

But minnie, minnie, beek ma haands afore da open braands."

"Minnie's jewel manna greet, but, lammie, come ta me,—

We mann lay at da cauld clods, or dan da fire wid dee;

But I sall beek da frost awa' fae dy twa bonny haands,

An' livin' colls 'ill mak' cauld clods dance up in lowin' taands."

O Bridders! dat's da only plan love kens to raise a lowe:

Lay-at a warm side till a cauld, an' troth ye'll see a towe!

O dünna shou'der aff püir sowls wi' frozen herts or haands,

For livin' colls 'ill mak cauld clods dance up in lowin' taands!

DA TWININ' O'T

I WATCHED her taese an' caird da 'oo',

    For, O, shü did it weel;

I watched her spin the wirsit tü

    Upo' da whirrin' wheel;

But whan shü broucht da sweerie doon

    Da *dooble raw* ta twine,

Aroond the wheel I danced a reel,

    I toucht it sae divine.

        Da twinin' o't, da twinin' o't,

          Der's naethin' like da twinin' o't,

        For love an' life ta man an' wife

          Ir i' da richt divinin' o't.

For let da 'oo' be e'er sae guid,

    Each hair withoot a flaw,

Da dooble stränd will only staand,

    Sae add anidder raw;

An' I was but a single treed,

    'At sairly did repine,

But hope arose upo' my woes

    Whane'er I saw her twine.

        Da twinin' o't, da twinin' o't,

            Der's naethin' like da twinin' ot,

            Content an' bliss, like lover's kiss,

            Ta tink upo' da twinin' o't.

Yet some hae lived da day ta rue

    Dey wirna single still;—

Wha link der treed wi' unspun 'oo'

    Der stockin' wears but ill.

Sae mind, young man, dy treed o' life,

    Be it or coorse or fine,

An' wale wi' care a triggy wife,

    A wife 'at düsna cline.

        Da clinin' o't, da clinin' o't,

          O dwine da graceless clinin' o't

          For hate an' strife to man an' wife

          Ir i' da fause-spun clinin' o't.

EXTRACTS FROM LETTERS

TO HIS BROTHER PETER

16th March 1885. — The soiree passed off very well. There were not so many people as last year however, but I think it was not so stiff, for the tables (instead of being in long rows necessitating your sitting as prim and decorous as old maids in a family pew) were placed *a la* the late pastor's Bible class, and you could move with the greatest of ease and pleasure from the one to the other … The speeches were fair … There was no report for the Literary, but C— gave a résumé of the session's work, and did it very well too. They wanted me to do it, but impromptu speechifying is not my forte …

On Saturday night I was at Gilbert Goudie, Esq.'s. It was a gathering of "Worthies"—"Surfaceman," George Stewart, L. J. Nicolson, and some Highland *littérateurs* and antiquaries. We had a very enjoyable evening. Mr. Goudie was exhibiting his northern trophies for inspection … "Surfaceman" is witty …

There was a splendid display of Aurora Borealis last night. The best I have seen for a long time. Did you not see it at Montrose?

24th May. — There was none of us out of town at all except Bob, who had been captured by some of — Choiristers, and he accordingly accommodated them, as they were short of eligible young men for the extraordinary stock-in-hand of female sweet singers …

The bonfires in honour of the Queen, or for the juvenile delight, were of course patronised in the evening by crowds, and a number of hampers, buckets, and things combustible were of course missed and mourned by many housekeepers, shopkeepers, and others …

There has not been a fully dry day since May came in, but as the poet sings, "It is not always May." What a blessing, I say!

21st July. — I think we are like to have a pleasant journey north. You can look for us passing Montrose, but we won't have time to pay you a visit …

I was at Mrs. — to tea on Saturday. Miss Grant Furley, L. J. Nicolson, and myself were all the "party," but we got on very well. I don't know whether you have seen Miss Furley's name before ... She has written many stories, essays, etc. etc.

28th September. — I am glad to hear of your success in the church bazaar lottery in securing £4 (cushion) for one shilling ... I don't exactly understand, though, how churches can run down betting and gambling in secular matters, and allow, or rather cherish, them in things ecclesiastical,—for, you know, what you did was really laying one to eighty on yourself in the race for the cushion. I do not want to moralise on it, nor object to gambling at all in a way, but what I refer to is the inconsistency of churches doing what they condemn in others ...

I noticed the *Scotsman's* article on the great Conservative demonstration—it was good. Alas, poor "Staffy"! A number of journals are at present running Chamberlain down for his last speech—they think his terms of accepting office too high—but it seems to me that the papers are rather misrepresenting the Right Hon. gentleman's meaning. They are good at that trick occasionally. Chamberlain, I believe, will have a large following in the next House of Commons, and there will of necessity be more of the advanced element in the Cabinet. We will shortly have "Auld Willie" among us. He's the boy that can rouse the country …

3rd May 1886. — I went to Glasgow on our Fast Day, and paid visits to a number of people … I spent a very enjoyable day, though I did not go to see many of the "sights." … People always have more attraction for me than scenery, even on a holiday, and the three times I have visited Glasgow I have stuck with the friends I have found in the smoke and din. If I want to go down the river I will have to do like Andrew—carry my supply of familiar faces with me, and then the scenery will be unparalleled.

5th May. — To-morrow the Exhibition here opens, and it is to be a grand affair … Six lasses are down from Shetland for the Exhibition … The jawbones of a whale are to form their triumphal arch of entrance, and their stall is to be draped with fishermen's nets … You would see the G. O. M.'s [Gladstone's] manifesto. It was magnificent …

28th June. — The most important thing at present here is politics, and we are having plenty of spouting.

14th July. — Bob is away in Shetland, and Andrew is studying the Home Rule question in the North of Ireland … Despite Scotland and Wales Mr. Gladstone will be in a minority in the new Parliament, and Home Rule is rebuffed in the meantime, but the hour is near nevertheless … I was more sorry for Trevelyan than for any other Unionist. He is a good Liberal on most points …

6th August. — I have had another boating excursion since we were at the Bridge of Dun … were out in Bob's pulling boat and enjoyed ourselves for about two hours on the firth. The sailing boat was out of order, or we would have had a sail …

Andrew is busy again trisecting an angle. That has never been done, and mathematicians say it can't be done—only Andrew thinks he has got it done. This is the tenth or twelfth time he has tried it, but on all *previous* occasions a flaw was found in the argument, and this one may be received *cum grano salis*.

19th November. — On Wednesday last I was appointed one of a deputation of two from the Edinburgh Orkney and Shetland Association to represent them at the Glasgow gathering in December, so it will be a fine excursion for me … Leonard Lyell, M.P. for the county, is to be in the chair, and I have no doubt there will be a good attendance of natives of the old Rock … I intended sending you the *Shetland Times* to-day with my article on the Shetland stall at the Exhibition, but I met William on my road to the office and he intercepted the paper. I am to get it back soon and will send it …

21st January 1887. — We have had rather an unpleasant experience in weather of late, two days never coming alike. I don't think I ever "mind" such rapid changes from fresh to frost and from frost to fresh, with all the different variations from rain to sunshine, as we have had since the year came in.

We have had a *fire* since last you heard from us. Mary had lit a fire for Andrew and his engineer-student when he should arrive, but the room filled with smoke on account of the vent not drawing properly; so Andrew calculated what was the requisite current of air necessary to draw that smoke up that "lum," and of course, when he had ascertained that, drew up the window the precise distance to allow this current access to the room. He then closed the room-door and betook himself to the kitchen. Now it happened that a certain policeman, Stewart to wit, was attracted in the street by sparks and flames flying out of a window on the top-flat, and so Mrs. L— next door was rung out to see if it was her place. She said it would be ours, and Mary and Andrew heard the bell ring with violence as they sat at ease in the kitchen. Mary opened the door and Mrs. L— and the Bobby confronted her, Mrs. L— white as a ghost, and crying, "Mary, hae ye a fire in your room? it's fleein' oot the window!" She waited for no reply but rushed ben, Mary and the Bobby at her heels—Mary almost frightened out of her wits by Mrs. L's appearance more than anything else. Sure enough they found the fire. The curtains at the window were consumed out of existence—i.e. all but some black ash. The woodwork was scorched and two chairs were burning. Andrew now (in the kitchen) had solved a problem in pure mathematics, and found that the room should now be clear of smoke, granting its primal density to have been equal to that from the funnel of a ship whose engines were of so many horse-power. Accordingly he went ben, and was surprised to find the result. On examination he found that he had forgot an important factor in his calculations, viz. a blazing gas-bracket in close proximity to the inflammable window curtain. "The best laid schemes o' mice and men gang aft agee [agley]." At this stage I arrived home from the office and learned the foregoing account. The policemen and the fireman (for the Bobby went for him) were in possession. But things quieted down. The crowd in the street dispersed—and we are going to send in our claim for Insurance! ...

We had Auntie Willa's four lasses down at tea last week ... Aunt Helen had a "Mrs. Anderson" party at Leith. There were seven Mrs. Andersons and no one else, and none else worth mentioning! ...

The Orkney and Shetland Annual Gathering comes off on 2nd February. Mr. George Stewart gave us an excellent Lecture on "The influences of city life on the race."

5th May. — I am sorry indeed to hear you had not been feeling so well as usual. I hope you are improving in health again ... Andrew has not been very well for some time ... He is perhaps to take a fortnight's holidays in the country before he goes on his Mediterranean voyage ... My little sketch of poor James John Johnston would appear yesterday in the *Shetland Times* ... To-day I had to read a paper on "Ishmael the outcast" to the Sabbath Morning Fellowship Association. Next Sunday Willie comes on with a paper on Isaac being offered up ...

I shall be glad to hear of your further acquaintance with Mr. Edwards ...

25th August. — I daresay you will be expecting a long record of my holiday experience in Shetland. I enjoyed it pretty well on the whole, and very well at times ... I had two days in Lerwick before going north. Mr. Sandison of the *Times* was very kind and friendly. I was at his house to tea on Sunday ... We had some music, vocal and instrumental ...

I also called on Mr. J. J. H. Burgess, a young Lerwick author ... The fine pier and esplanade, which the

Lerwick folks have now got, are a great improvement … But I think the little town is not quite so picturesque now with an esplanade between it and the sea from whose waters the houses actually rose in former years; so that the Lerwick man could hang his pot on the fire and sit in the window and draw just the right quantity of sillocks for the pot! …

I went to Fetlar … As we steamed along towards Tresta I was shown the Hughsons' house … Hubie is what it is called, and soon the Hubie boat was seen under sail … the Hughsons in the boat … Soon they were aboard wanting to know if I was going to land, and if not to make me! … I enjoyed Fetlar very much. With rifle and fowling-piece we went out shooting, doing some damage to sea-gulls, scarfs and rocks. One of the Hughsons shot a seal, and they had him skinned …

The weather was more broken when I was in Unst, and I did not see so much as I would have liked … I fished the burn and got a few trout … I went to Muness with a picnic party, in the big flit-boat. Andrew Anderson was in command … Muness Castle was duly inspected, particularly the coat-of-arms stone above the door. A certain Muness man wanted to procure it for a hearthstone! It was of no use where it was—in fact was just lost, he thought.

23rd September. — Married life has not made a great change on Willie (this was a point open to observation). He is still a great critic and rebuker of all devious ways. He corrects mother for saying "skoit" because no such word is found in the dictionary of good English; and mother and I are the only pair he ever saw drinking a cup of tea, when very hot, after the manner of a young calf. Willie is still a prolific writer … Willie is good and sound, orthodox and Tory … When I shall have lost all of the child I think I shall have grown old, though I should not be gray-headed. This would be a very sad and cold world without children and child-hearted men …

I am sorry to tell you that Andrew is no better— indeed, I should say much weaker … He is just away to a skeleton, and has to be carried to and from bed. He is so helpless. The students are of course not coming to the house now, except when one calls asking for him. Yesterday he complained of it being so wearisome having to sit still … Poor boy, it must be, and I feel very sorry for him, but he keeps up a wonderful heart ...

I hope he may pull through, but I fear—O Peter, I could hardly stand it if he were to go, which God forbid! ... I hope you are keeping well yourself. I am keeping "fairish," still not clear in the throat—but as I have invested in a big bottle of cod liver oil which I am applying copiously I hope to clear out Mr. Cough and guard against him in future ...

10th October. — You will have got my note of last night containing the brief notice of dear Andrew's death. He was quite conscious till the last, and Mother, Mary, Bob and I were round him as he departed. He was quite peaceful and resigned, as he had long told us, to depart from this earth to a brighter and better. "Jesus, receive my spirit" were the last words he uttered ... I read your letter to him, but he was too weak, and not able to speak in response. He just gave, as it were, a silent consent to all you said ... Mother is bearing up wonderfully ... and for myself I may say the anxiety that had weighed heavily on me for some time, and the pain at seeing Andrew suffering, passed away, and though I had to weep I felt somehow eased …

27th November. — Things are moving on slowly with us here … I have not been out much for some time, and I have not paid a visit to any of our friends since our brother's departure. My cold is not better … it is very persistent in sticking to me. "These things ought not to be."

Mother was at church last Sunday after a protracted absence, and she and I after service went down to Warriston to where Andrew lies …

The Literary opens on Tuesday … I am not down in the syllabus. Willie, I notice, is down for an essay on "The unreasonableness of so-called free thought."

I have received No. 4 of the *Orkney and Shetland American*, containing on the front page an effusion mine … We have had a big meeting of Liberals in Edinburgh, which was a great success … I considered it advisable not to go … We will likely have a stiff contest in the West Division in February … Ireland is being completely muddled …

9th November. — I have put in an application for the position of Assistant-Librarian to the Free Library … I fear I have not much chance … they want, I believe, trained Librarians …

24th November. — We are all pretty well except myself … I am confined to the house. I had to come home from work Wednesday last week, and am still to be from work a while—short, I hope … I hope you are still keeping well. Dr. B— says you are not very strong and should take care …

7th December. — I am keeping a little better, and am marching out with the height of the day, but I am not at all able as yet to resume work, and I fear I shall yet have more time of idleness, before then …

TO HIS FRIEND CHARLES NICOL

August 1886. — But poets sing as fancy leads, and if you see any gushing effusion of grief for a lost wife with my signature subjoined you must not run away with the belief that I have lost what I have never yet found.

October. — I have not courted the Muses to any great extent, and the Muses are sometimes more shy than more earthly maids … I think I have lost some of the buoyancy of spirit that bore me up in the old days.

March 1887. — I am sorry to say our friend J. J. J. is unwell again. Poor chap! His left lung is affected, and I doubt he will have a hard battle with the last enemy … Of course the rider of the Pale Horse always wins in the end with the strongest of us.

Good Friday. — Our poor friend J. J. J. is very weak … the best of him lies in the past now … My brother William has just returned from a trip to London. He wrote a paper for the *Police Journal*, "On and off Duty," … read his paper at a meeting of Police

Delegates in Exeter Hall … he heard the debate on the Irish Question in the Commons. Mr. Labouchere was the speaker, or rather the *orator* he heard. The Speaker in the Commons is the man who does not speak!

May. — The Muse is not always flying at the same height, and is apt at times, even with the master-bards, to sink into the depths … to wit, when Tennyson wrote his Jubilee ode!

December. — My mother, I am happy to tell you, is yet spared to us, and I hope will be for some time to come. But trouble has been in our family since I wrote to you last, and we have sustained a heavy loss in the death of my brother Andrew … He passed away peacefully, and we laid him to rest in Warriston Cemetery … We miss him much, but hope to meet again … I am weak and languid, and in a "useless" condition … I am not in a desponding mood however, but happy in mind. My motto is "Aye bear a lichtsome heart." … I have not had much inclination or time for poetry lately. Life has pressed its cares too heavily for that.

GLOSSARY OF SHETLAND TERMS

Gilbert Goudie

NOTE

To the lamented author's countrymen the peculiarities of language in the specially native pieces in the collection will present little or no difficulty. But it has seemed desirable, in the judgment of the editor, that a glossary should be provided for the use of readers who may not be acquainted with the dialect, and I have gladly undertaken the duty at her request.

Apart from the purely local terms, the pieces contain many words of current English, which are so disguised in their phonetic rendering, according to northern usage, as probably to seem uncouth and unintelligible to south-country readers. One of the most fruitful factors in this disguising is the aversion in Shetland, as on the Continent, to the pronunciation in the English method of *th*, which is usually modified into *d* or *t*. In this way *then* becomes "den," *that* becomes "dat," *thing* "ting," *thought* "toucht," and the like. Such words as these, though of no intrinsic value as dialect variations, have been included in the glossary, in order to prevent misunderstanding or confusion.

Some of the pieces which appeared in Scottish newspapers affect the Scottish dialect. There are also a number of words occurring in the specially native pieces which may at first sight seem to be Scotticisms, but which are not necessarily to be regarded as importations from Scotland. These are usually differentiations and coincidences common to all the languages which acknowledge their derivation from the old mother tongues of the Teutonic and Scandinavian north. The best preserved form of the latter is in the ancient literature of Iceland, which is referred to in the glossary as Old Northern, abbreviated as *O.N.*; *Dan.* representing Danish; and *Su.-G.* Sueo-Gothic.

As regards pronunciation, the main exceptional feature is the letter *U*, which, when marked with the diæresis (*ü*) has the same phonetic value as *ö* in German and Danish, and of *eu* in French, for which there is no exact equivalent in English.

The native Shetland pieces are conceived in vigorous and expressive vernacular, without straining or affectation, and exhibit a close affinity to the Norse, which, once universal, struggled on in the islands for ages, and has left with us, at the present day, these interesting traces which deserve to be treasured as echoes of a dying tongue.

GILBERT GOUDIE

EDINBURGH, *March* 1888.

GLOSSARY

Aalie, pet, home-nourished, fed by the hand. (Old Northern, *ala*, to bring up, nourish.)

The true spirit and meaning of this Shetland word *aalie*, and of *bül* and *will*, which also occur in these poems, is well brought out by comparison of the passage in Ezekiel xxxiv. 15, rendered in the Revised Version—

"I myself will feed my sheep, and I will cause them to lie down, saith the Lord God; I will seek that which was lost, and will bring again that which was driven away."

In the Icelandic this reads—

"*Eg vil siálfur* ala *mina saudi, og Eg vil* bœla *thá, segir Drottin: Eg vil uppleita thann glatada, og leida aptur thann sem* villist."

Using the appropriate Shetland terms, this may be literally rendered—

"I will myself *aalie* my sheep, and I will *bül* them, saith the Lord: I will seek for that which was hurt, and will lead back that which is *willt.*"

In comparison with the idea here of "*büling*" the sheep (putting them to rest in night-quarters), the English, "causing them to lie down," conveys but a poor and imperfect meaning, if any meaning at all; while to *aalie* them (to feed, nourish, bring them up), and to bring back those that are *willt* (wandered, lost, strayed), is very fine. Milton in *Lycidas* presents a telling picture of the faithless shepherd, to whom—

"The hungry sheep look up and are not fed."

But this seems to be surpassed in expressiveness by the touching lines in these simple Shetland lays—

"We leuk to Dee [the Almighty] like *aalie* sheep."

And again—

"Lord, caa' me hame Dy ain Christ's *aalie*-lamb."

The idea here is, that the sheep, the lamb, are not only pet, nourished, fed, but that they are, or were, weak, helpless, orphaned, wholly dependent for both care and nourishment.

Aert, earth.

Aet, eat.

Anidder, another.

Ase, ashes.

At's, that is.

Aze, blazing fire. (O.N. *eisa*, glowing embers.)

Baak, cross-beam in a cottage. (Anglo-Saxon, *balca*; Ger. *balken*.)

Baess, Baste, beasts, farm-cattle. (Dan. *beest*.)

Bank, peat. [*specifically, where peat is cut*]

Bedd, abode, resided. Past tense of *bide*. (O.N. *bida*, to stay, wait.)

Beek, to caress with warmth.

Bere, or **Bigg**, the native coarse barley. (Dan. *byg*, barley.)

Bere-burstin-crül, a small cake (*crül*) of coarse barley (*bere*) ground after having been dried in a kettle, instead of in a kiln in the usual way, and baked upon or before the fire (*burstin*). Edmondston gives another definition: "*Crule*—meal mixed with cold water and eaten raw, with a lump of butter in the middle of it." The Icelandic or Old Northern, *kræla*, to stir, from which the word may probably be derived, seems to harmonise with this latter definition.

Berg, O.N. *bjarg*, cliff, precipice; Ger. *berg*, mountain. Applied in the text to icebergs.

Bewillt, an intensified form of wilt. (See **Will**, to miss one's way. O.N. *villa*, the same.)

Bide, to stay, abide. (O.N. *bida*.)

Big, to build. (Dan. *bygge*.)

Bit, but.

Blue-finned, blue-moulded.

Bodies, grown-up persons.

Bonns, bones.

Booed, bowed.

Bress, brass.

Brochs, the circular towers of the early "Pictish" inhabitants, at one time very numerous, but now all in ruins, except the single example in the island of Mousa.

Brods, boards.

Brook, brük, broke.

Brü, water in which meat, etc., has been boiled. (Akin to English, *brew*; Anglo-Saxon, *breovan*.)

Bruck, broken fragments.

Brünnie, round, thick, small oatmeal cake. (O.N. *bruni*, a burning.)

Büdie, straw basket of somewhat different shape from the *keshie*, but used and carried in much the same way. (Provincial Danish, *bóddel*, the same meaning.)

Buggy-flay, to flay an animal so as to leave the skin entire, to form a *buggie*, or skin bag. (Dan. *bug*.)

Bül, a sheltered resting-place. (O.N. *ból*, the lair or lying-place of beasts or cattle.) See note to **Aalie**.

Bulgit, bulged.

Burstin, corn ground into meal after being dried in a kettle instead of in a kiln. (Derivation uncertain.)

By, besides.

By, past.

Caa', call (also to drive).

Caird, card.

Cap, bowl (made of wood). Su.-G. *koppa* (akin to cup).

Carcage, carcass.

Chunt, blow, stroke (of a pick).

Cline, to cover with butter, grease, or such like. (O.N. *klina*, to smear; in modern Icelandic, to daub.)

Clods (of peat). [*specifically, small pieces*]

Coll, coal (applied to burning peat).

Corbie, raven.

Craig, throat. (Teutonic, *kraeghe*.)

Crü, in the island of Unst, and probably elsewhere in the north of Shetland, this word, as in the text (Auld Maunsie's Crü), is used for the small, usually round, walled enclosure for rearing young plants. In the south of Shetland the term for this is *crub*; while *crü*, as in Iceland, is the term applied to a pen into which sheep are driven for shearing or other purposes. (O.N. *kró*; Dan. *kro*, a small pen or fence.)

Crü-steead wis aert-kent, the foundation of the crü was earth kent, that is, was universally known.

Cruggin', cowering.

Crül. (See **Bere-burstin-crül**.)

Cüle, cool.

Cüt, cud. (Anglo-Saxon, *cud*, what is chewed.)

Da, the.

Dan, than.

Darg, work, labour (believed to be originally an abbreviation of *day-werk*).

Dat, that.

Dee, thee, you.

Deir, Der, their.

Deks, dykes (stone walls).

Dem, them.

Den, then.

De'r, they are.

Dere, there.

Dess, a hay-stack. (Cambro-Britannic or Welsh, *das*, a heap of grain; Teutonic, *tas*, the same.)

Dey, they.

Dey'd, they would.

Dicklin', recklessly trampling.

Drēm, dream.

Du, thou.

Dü, do.

Dy, thy.

Elbucks, elbows. (Anglo-Saxon, *elboga*.)

Ene, one.

Ert, direction (of the wind). Scottish, *airt*.

Fae, from. (O.N. *frá*; Dan. *fra*; Scottish, *frae*.)

Fann, snow-wreath. (O. N. *fönn*, a heap of snow.) In Norway *folge-fonn*, the name of a glacier.

Fanns-wir-scoomed, snow-wreaths were "scummed" or cleared off.

Farles, properly the fourth part of a thin cake; here (*The laddie he was blate*) used apparently in a more general sense for *eatables*. (Anglo-Saxon, *feorth-dael*, fourth share.)

Ferlies, wonders. (Anglo-Saxon, *faerlic*.) Niceties, presents; used perhaps ambiguously with the preceding word **Farles**.

Ferry-ring, fairy circle.

Fey, afraid.

Fiel, hill. (Dan. *fjeld*.)

Fiord, firth. (O.N. *fjordr*; Dan. *fjord*.)

Flytin', scolding (also Scottish; Anglo-Saxon, *flitan*, to brawl).

Fram, forth, outside, away, strange. (Dan. *frem*.)

Fremd, Fremmit, stranger, foreign, alien, strangers. (Dan. *fremmed*.)

Füle, foolish.

Gaarsed, caused. The past tense of *gar* (Old English and Scottish), to make, to cause, to do, equivalent to O.N. *göra*; Dan. *gjöre*, a word common to all the Scandinavian north.

Gaed, Güid, Güde, went.

Geng, go. (O.N. *ganga*; Anglo-Saxon, *gangan*; Danish, Norwegian, Swedish, *gange* or *go*; Scottish, gang.) **Geen**, gone.

Glowrin', staring (Scottish).

Goit, threshold. (O.N. *gata*; Dan. *gade*, way or road.)

Gorsty-girse, gorse grass.

Graff, grave. (O. N. *gröf;* Ger. *grabe*; Dan. *grav*, Swed. *graf*.)

Groint, grunt.

Gyaun, going.

Ha', hall (here a cave by the sea).

Haaf, deep-sea fishing. (O.N. and Swed. *haf*, the ocean; Dan. *hav*, a very common word in Northern literature, but unknown to English or Scottish.)

Haarled oot, dragged slowly out.

Had, hold.

Hadden, holden or holding (in *sheep-hadden wa'*).

Hairst, harvest (often pronounced *haist*). O.N. *haust*; Dan. and Swed. *höst*.

Hame, heim, home. (O.N. *heimr*; Ger. *heim*; Dan. *hjem*; Swed. *hem*.)

Hedder-cowe, heather-cowe, a tuft of heather. [*specifically, a dried-out heather branch possibly used as tinder*]

Heilded, moved or passed over to one side.

Helyer, a cave by the sea. (O.N. *hellir*.)

Hert, heart. (O.N. *hjarta*; Anglo-Saxon, *heorte*; Dan. *hjerte*.)

Hert-stane, hearth-stone.

Heth, an exclamation—indeed! truly!

Hill-baess could claw, cattle grazing in the hill could scrape and *paw* with their feet.

Hirsie, move (Scottish). Anglo-Saxon, *hirstlan*.

Hock, dig. (Scottish, *howk*.)

Howe, a tumulus, mound. (O.N. *haugr*; Dan. *höj*.) Black Chiel's Howe = Satan's dwelling-place.

Huggit, hugged.

Huggy-staff, a stout short stick with pointed hook at end, used for *striking into* fish in hauling them on board. (O.N. *högg*, a stroke or blow, especially with an edged weapon; *höggva*, to strike.)

Idder, other.

Iggit, incited. (Dan. *egge*, to incite; Scottish, *egg*.)

Ir, are.

Keek, to look by stealth, to peep. (Su.-G. *kika*.)

Kep, cap.

Keshie (sometimes spelt *cassie*, *cazzie*, and *caishey*), the native straw creel or basket, carried on the back, or slung across a horse, one on either side, pannier-like. (O.N. and Dan. *kassi*, a case, box, or creel.)

Kruipins, persons, individuals, bodies. (O.N. *kroppr*, Ger. *kropf*, Dan. *krop*; Swed. *kropp*, body.)

Kyunnen, rabbit. (Dan. *kanin*; Old English, *conyng*.)

Laef, leaf.

Laek, like.

Laigh, low (Scottish).

Langsome, slow, tardy, lazy. (Dan. *langsom*.)

Lede, load.

Lempit, limpet.

Less, alas.

Liftin', cattle are said to be *liftin'* or *in liftin'* when they are so much reduced by poor feeding as to be unable to rise, and to require to be lifted.

Lowe, flame. (O.N. *logi*; Ger. *lohe*; Dan. *lue*.)

Lowin', burning brightly, blazing.

Madram, fun, folly.

Magnie, the familiar form of the Old Northern personal name Magnus, derived from Charlemagne (Carolus Magnus).

Mam, mother. (Teutonic, *mamme*; Latin, *mamma*.)

Mann, must. (O.N. *mun*; Scottish, *maun*.)

Moorit, a brownish colour (in wool); possibly connected with the colour of moorland earth. (Norse, *myre*, in which the pronunciation is somewhat similar.)

Mooth, mouth.

Mooty-ting, mite (of a) thing.

Muildy, earthy, mouldy.

Nedder, Nidder, neither.

Neist, next.

No, not.

Nord, Nort, north.

Oo, wool.

Oor, hour.

Oot, out.

Oot-o-daeks, in the hill-common, outside the township dykes.

Oxterin', holding under the arm. (Anglo-Saxon, *oxtan*.)

Paet, peat.

Pechts, the "Picts."

Peerie, little (origin uncertain). Edmondston gives Norse, *piren*, as cognate.

Pellat, ragged, tattered. (Dan. *pialtet*.)

Pickit, picked away.

Pooer, power.

Purlin', fumbling, groping.

Raabin', falling, tumbling down. (O.N. *hrapa*, the same.)

Rade, rode.

Raikin dogs, wandering, stray dogs.

Raikin, Raikit, reaching, stretching over, *i.e.* walking.

Rigg, backbone. (Swed. Gothic, and Old Dan. *rygg*.)

Riggin-tree, roof-tree (*riggin*, ridge, akin to *rigg*, backbone).

Ringed, encircled.

Riskin', cutting, tearing up.

Ro, a poor weak animal, in a helpless or dying state.

Rodd, road.

Rooin', plucking wool off sheep instead of shearing. (Dan. *rove*, to take away, rob.)

Roosty, rusty.

Rül, a young horse.

Sain, to bless, consecrate. In the text, to guard, to preserve. (Ger. *segnen*, to bless.)

Scad, scald.

Schapter, chapter.

Schime, chime.

Scoit, peep. (Dan. *skotte*, to steal a glance, cast a sly look.)

Scoored, scoured.

Sew, sowed.

Shaef, sheaf.

Sheek, cheek (side of the fire).

Sheep-hadden, sheep-holden (*i.e.* capable of resisting the encroachment of sheep, which in Shetland leap like goats).

Shooskie, according to Edmondston this term is sometimes applied to the devil, as an epithet of disrespect. (Dan. *siasket*, nasty, slovenly, sloppy.)

Shorded, fixed, placed, propped up (like a boat secured on land by props on either side).

Showed, chewed.

Showins, food (*chewings*).

Shü, she.

Shure, shore [*cut*]

Shure his tap, shore his crown.

Simmer, summer.

Sin', since.

Sixaerin, six-oared boat. (O.N. *sex-aeringr*, in which form it occurs in the *Orkneyinga Saga*.)

Skyaag, small turf-house for geese. ("Skyaagin' da geese.")

Slap, a broken-down passage in a dyke. *Slaps* were also known in Scotland at a time when the conditions of country life, townships, enclosures, appear to have been in some degree similar to what still prevails in Shetland—

"... The lang Scots miles,

The mosses, waters, *slaps* and stiles." [BURNS, 'Tam o' Shanter']

Smit, to infect. **Smit**, infected. (Anglo-Saxon, *smitan*.)

Smored, drowned, smothered. (Anglo-Saxon, *smoran*.)

Smuck, woollen knitted slipper. (Akin to English, *smock*.)

Soond, sound. (Dan. *sund*, a narrow passage of sea.)

Sooth, south.

Spaek, speak.

Spunkie, spark of fire. (Gaelic, *sponc*, tinder or touchwood.)

Spüre. (Definition not very certain. *Güde spüre da heim folk* is used to express the wish that good luck may befall them.)

Staagin, walking lazily. **Staagit**, walked. (O.N. *staka*, to stagger; Dan. *stage*, to push, shove along.)

Staarn, star. (O.N. *stjarna*, a word common to all Indo-Germanic languages, Cleasby-Vigfusson.)

Staarn, stern [*of a boat*]

Stack, a rock in the sea, usually high or pointed. (O.N. *stakkr*; Dan. *stak*, a stack.)

Stank, ditch. (Su.-G. *stanc*.)

Stark, rigid. (O.N. *sterkr*; Dan. *stærk*, strong, a common word in Teutonic languages.)

Steead, Steethe, foundation, bottom. (O.N. *stadr*, Dan. *sted*, a place, spot.)

Stentin, stretching.

Stottit, staggered.

Strik, strike. **Strick some teck**, cut heather-tops.

Stroopie, tea-pot with a *stroup* or spout.

Süt, Shüt, soot.

Swarf, swoon. (Akin to O.N. *svarfa*, reflex, to turn upside down.)

Sweerie, the box containing the reels upon which thread is wound preparatory to being twisted into double or triple cord.

Sweery, lazy. (Anglo-Saxon, *svere*.)

Ta, to.

Taand, a burning brand of peat. (O.N. *tandri*, fire.)

Taing, a tongue of land projecting into the sea. (Dan. *tange*.)

Taise, tease.

Tap, top.

Tautie, potato.

Tidder, the other.

Ting, thing.

Tink, think.

Tooer, tower.

Toom, thumb.

Toonmals, Tunmals, grass land adjoining the *tún*, farm, or township. (O.N. *tún*; Dan. *maal*, measure, dimension.)

Touchts, Toughts, thoughts.

Towe, thaw.

Troagin', trudging.

Treed, thread.

Triggy, trim, tidy.

Troo, through.

Trows, goblins resident in the hills or retired places. (Dan. *trold*.)

Truck, to trample about. (Dan. *trykke*.)

Tü, too.

Üle, (of heat) glow, warmth.

Veesek, a song or ballad. (O.N. *visa*; Ger. *weise*; Dan. *visa*, a strophe, stanza.)

Voar, spring. (O. N. *vár*; Dan. *vaar*.)

Vod, empty, unoccupied, void (Edmondston).

Voe, an arm of the sea. (O.N. *vágr*; Dan. *vaag*, pronounced like *vae*.)

Vord, hill. (O. N. *varda*; Dan. *varde*.)

Waddered, weathered.

Wale, to choose. (Su.-G. *waelia*.) Common also in Scottish, e.g. (taking down the Bible)—

"He *wales* a portion with judicious care,

And 'Let us worship God,' he says with solemn air."

(BURNS' *Cottar's Saturday Night*.)

Wan, one.

Wastral, outcast, prodigal.

Watter, water.

Whan, Whin, when.

Wharried, quarried.

Wheer, queer [*unusual*]

Wheyg, young cow.

Whillie, the smallest size of Shetland boat.

Wid, would.

Widden, wooden.

Will, to miss one's way, to wander. (O.N. *villa*, to go astray.) See note to **Aalie**.

Wir, our.

Wir, were.

Wirsit, worsted.

Wis, us.

Wis, was.

Wiss, wish.

Wrate, written.

Wup, twist, binding. (Mæso-Gothic, *waib-jan*, to surround.)

Wy, way.

Yall, yell.

Yett, a gate.

Yowe, ewe (Scottish).

NOTES ON THE SECOND EDITION

The original text has been preserved in the new edition, with period spelling and phrasing such as "every one" and "for ever", except in cases where the first edition appears to contain an error or oversight. These are few, but noticeable. I will note them here.

In the Shetland dialect poems, there are some instances where the conjunction "and" appears in its English form as opposed to "an' ", which is by far the more dominant. Whether this variation was in the original manuscript or not is unknown, but it is quite possible these were merely oversights on the part of a typesetter more used to standard English, gone unnoticed by the editor—that errors were occasionally made in this matter is obvious from the solitary use of "an" without apostrophe, where sense makes clear that "and" / "an' " was intended: "Ta langsome legs an elbucks tü— " ('Auld Maunsie's Crü'). A similar issue arises with the English "when", occurring three times in the same poem, as opposed to the dialect "whan" which appears eight times.

This intrusion of the English form is most apparent in the title 'Livin' Colls and (sic) Cauld Clods'. While some little variation may be tolerable, even expected, so noticeable a trend is less so. Believing these to be errors in the printing, I have standardised these occasional English intrusions of "and" and "when" into the otherwise dominant dialect form, on the assumption that this is, as Mrs. Saxby says in defence of her own editorial interventions, something Basil Anderson himself would have done had he lived to supervise publication in book form.

Aside from these matters, changes are very few: the quotation from 'Livin' Colls an' Cauld Clods' in Mrs. Saxby's introduction gives a hyphen between "lay at" which is not present in the poem itself. I read this as a compound verb phrase, rather than verb and preposition, and so have added the hyphen in the poem, presuming that to be the mistake; secondly, I amended what appears to be an error in punctuation in 'A Cry From The Poor', where we find a comma though sense and verse form suggest a full stop; also, where the third line of 'Fragment' appears to contain an error, giving "To' " while sense suggests "Tho' "; besides these few interventions, in one or two cases, I have added a brief additional note to an entry in Goudie's glossary, in italics in square brackets.

The original verse forms have been reproduced in the vast majority of cases. However, in the first edition there were a small number of cases in particular poems where text ran over onto subsequent lines, so that the visual aspect of the verse was adversely affected—which would not, I assume, have been present in manuscript. We have endeavoured to eliminate these overspills in order to better illustrate the skill of the verse forms, which on occasion has required a slight modification of indented lines—though the original formal relations indicated by the first edition have been preserved, in principle, even there.

Unfortunately, the poem which suffers most from the rather cramped presentation of the first edition is the 'masterpiece',

'Auld Maunsie's Crü'—continuation of verses through page-breaks is awkward, and makes it impossible to be certain whether the end of the poem should be read as one single stanza of 20 lines, or two of 10. The first possibility is not improbable, as stanza length varies considerably in what precedes from 6 to 18 lines, and this being the conclusion, the temptation to extend the verse may have won out. Sense runs through the page-break, suggesting the continuous longer stanza—but visually the first edition inadvertently suggests separation. We cannot be sure without Anderson's scrapbook, but given the emphatic manner in which other stanzas end, I'm inclined to assume the former—which presents us with the same problem the original typesetter may have encountered, of a long stanza and where to break it. I have settled on a compromise which shifts page at a point where sense corresponds, not in mid-sentence, in this notional 20-line long stanza, but otherwise have attempted to show the versification in a clearly unified visual manner, true to what I believe the original text to have been.

RAJ.

SUBSCRIBERS

This series could not have been published without the invaluable assistance of those who subscribed via a crowdfunding platform. The series editor and publisher would like to acknowledge their help with their heartfelt thanks, and, in time-honoured tradition, with public salutation in the following list:

Hazel Anderson; Helen Bowell; Eileen Brooke-Freeman; Wilma Cluness; Eleanor Coghill; Laura Dalgarno-Platt; Christine de Luca; Alistair Hamilton; Brian Holton; John Hunter; Kareen Hunter; Nancy Hunter; Joanne Jamieson; Karen Jamieson; Catherine Jeromson; Angus Johnson; Ingri Johnson; June Johnson; Magnus Laurenson; Fiona Macinnes, Morag McGill; Duncan McLean; Paul Manson; Graham March; Tim Morrison; Jim & Rosabel Nicolson; Elizabeth Park; Catherine Post; Neil Ritch; Margaret Roberts; Sheila Robertson; Carla Sassi; Magnus Shearer; Jane Shouesmith-Black; Beryl Smith; Dale Smith; Ingrid Smith; Janet Smith; Jen Stout; Linda Sutherland; Marsali Taylor; Ann & Ian Thomson; Margaret Tong; Jean Urquhart; Kenny Watt; Elizabeth Williamson.

Robert Alan Jamieson & Mike Walmer, April 2021

Lightning Source UK Ltd.
Milton Keynes UK
UKHW012037270521
384501UK00001B/74

9 780648 920472